NCAA Baseball Rules
in
Black and White:
2019 – 2020

Jim Bettencourt

BLUE RIVER PRESS
Indianapolis, Indiana

Dedication

This book is dedicated to thousands of incredibly committed and hard-working men and women umpires who are always striving to improve their profession in order to make the game of baseball even better.

NCAA Baseball Rules in Black and White: 2019 – 2020
Copyright © Jim Bettencourt 2019

Published by Blue River Press
Indianapolis, Indiana
www.brpressbooks.com

Distributed by Cardinal Publishers Group
A Tom Doherty Company, Inc.
www.cardinalpub.com

All rights reserved under International and Pan-American Copyright Conventions.

No part of this book may be reproduced, stored in a database or other retrieval system, or transmitted in any form, by any means, including mechanical, photocopy, recording or otherwise, without the prior written permission of the publisher.

ISBN: 978-1-68157-151-5

Cover Design: Scott Lohr
Book Design: Dave Reed
Cover Photo: Dreamstime
Editor: Dani McCormick

Printed in the United States of America

10 9 8 7 6 5 4 3 2 1 19 20 21 22 23 24 25 26 27 28

Contents

Foreword

Every year around mid-June, I'm reminded "why" I started umpiring baseball. The pure and simple answer, I love youth baseball! I loved playing it, I loved coaching it, and I loved watching my kids play it. Like many others in our avocation, my umpiring began at the Little League level. One day our Little League program needed bodies to umpire and I was willing to give it a try, as my two boys had recently aged out of the program. Now not only am I officiating youth baseball, I get to enjoy umpiring upper levels of baseball as well.

This year, I enjoyed working yet another Little League All-Star tournament in our community. On this particular day the baseball complex had four games being played at one time. Between innings during one of my games, I briefly scanned the other three fields and had a Deja vu of my own past personal umpire experiences. Dads, multiple dads that is, from area Little League programs out on these fields umpiring district all-star baseball games in their first or second season of umpiring. These same dads, who in years past had been Little League coaches, board members, and

league presidents, all out there giving back to the game at this level of baseball and having a great time doing so. This will be the first time for some of these
dads to find out what the complexities of umpiring are really all about. They will soon know what it feels like to either kick or get a call right. They will quickly learn the extreme importance of knowing the exact definition of a ruling. The importance of correctly applying the ruling during a game and being able to articulate it correctly to a coach.

I am well aware of what these new umpires will be going through as I have just completed my sixth season of umpiring, first year as a basketball official plus twenty years as a football referee. In recent years, I typically umpire 80 to 100 baseball games per season. To date in my umpire career, this means over 100 Little League games; over 100 lower-level college games; over 250 high school games and a Texas State Tournament semi-final at Disch-Falk Field in Austin. In addition, a sprinkling of a half-dozen, AA-MiLB, fill-in-umpire games for good measure. I thoroughly enjoy calling every level of baseball that I have experienced so far. At the upper levels that I am now working, the importance of a correct ruling is even more critical. Having a rule-book-resource that quickly and accurately provides a pre-game review, or post-game confirmation is extremely valuable to me.

We all share a common trait in the officiating community, we can't stand it when we make an incorrect ruling. Nine out of ten times, I know when I get a call wrong, and it eats at me like crazy. There is nothing that a coach, player or fan can say to me when I make the wrong call, that's worse than my own self-criticism. You know the feeling, don't you? You replay "the video" in your mind over and over again beating yourself up. Truth be known, the language in baseball rule books is the main cause of errant rulings and the biggest hurdle for most every umpire to master.

From a first-time umpire dad in Little League all the way up to the Major Leagues, we umpires are constantly studying to improve our rule book knowledge. Rule book language is an enormous barrier, especially for newer umpires, but it challenges even the most experienced officials. This is why I strongly recommend *Baseball Rules in Black and White.* These series of books have provided me with clarity with the most poorly worded rulings in the high school (NFHS) and college (NCAA) baseball rule books. The information in these books will quickly empower any umpire with baseball rule knowledge in an easy to read Basic English, easy to retain and apply format. Nothing will accelerate a beginning umpire's confidence or expand a veteran's knowledge like *Baseball Rules in Black and White.*

—Dal Watson

Dal Watson is from Odessa/Midland Texas has officiate football for twenty years, he currently a tri-sport official The last six years he has worked baseball, with four of those years working at the Junior College level.

Introduction

Welcome to *NCAA Baseball Rules in Black and White: 2019 – 2020*. This edition has been created through a collaboration of dedicated, knowledgeable, highly respected and professional baseball umpires, assignors, and rule editors.

In our third year we are ecstatic to present our *NCAA Baseball Rules in Black and White: 2019 – 2020* with an awesome new look, expanded content, and continued reader friendly format. We are committed to always improving content and format, which strengthens the reader's quest for improved baseball rule knowledge.

This edition is an enhanced learning resource for frequently called and complex rules of college baseball. By enhancing baseball rule book language and format, we are improving the value to the reader while supporting the actual source of those rulings. NCAA, Division I, and College World Series umpire, Mr. Billy Haze, has defined the Baseball Rules in Black and White series as the "CliffsNotes for official baseball rule books".

Baseball Rules in Black and White accomplishes this in several ways. Related components of an initial ruling are listed on the same page in logical order of sequence. Exceptions and examples that apply are also included with an initial ruling. Finding the ruling you need is easy as reading the alphabetical table of contents.

This unique, multi-beneficial format and content are only available in Baseball Rules in Black and White. *NCAA Baseball Rules in Black and White: 2019 – 2020* complements the NCAA baseball rule book by providing official NCAA rule and page numbers with most every ruling. This allows the reader to quickly find and cross-reference the official ruling.

We have spent three years and hundreds of hours developing these books while working with dozens of umpires, assignors, instructional chairs, rule interpreters, and rule editors from across the country. These are just few of the reasons we believe you will quickly see why Baseball Rules in Black and White is "A better way to learn the rules of baseball."

This book is dedicated to thousands of incredibly committed and hard-working men and women umpires who are always striving to improve their profession in order to make the game of baseball even better.

An effective baseball rules resource should take you directly to a rule, use straightforward language to convey a clear and decisive interpretation, list all the ruling options, all while retaining accuracy. We are positive you will find *NCAA Baseball Rules in Black and White: 2019 – 2020* to be that resource!

Balk

Infractions by pitchers are common and it is important to know what constitutes a balk, but also what it is not a balk. A balk in baseball is one of the most subtle, obvious, and random infractions in the game today, so much so that at every level of the game of baseball, few if any can agree on whether a balk infraction did or did not happen. This illuminates the importance of clearly being able to understand the exact definitions of the rulings for a balk at each specific level of play in order to correctly call a balk during a game.

Definition of a Balk

- An illegal act is committed by the pitcher with runners on base.

Rule 2: Section: 3: Page 21.

Penalty: The ball becomes dead and all runners advance one base.

Rule 9: Section: 3-m, Penalty, Page 88, 89.

Balks Followed by a Wild Throw or Pitch

- A balk is immediately followed by a wild throw to a base by the pitcher that allows the runners to advance to or beyond the base they were entitled to. The balk is still acknowledged.

  Results:

  1. The umpires will call a balk in the usual manner, but will not call time until all play has ceased.
  2. When a balk happens with no additional play, the pitch is nullified and the pitch count reverts to what it was prior to the balk.

  Rule 8: Section: 3-m-3), Note 2, Page 92.

- When only the runners advance to or beyond the base from a wild pitch after a balk, the balk is still acknowledged.

  Note: The runner may advance past the base award at the runner's own risk.

  Rule 9: Section: 3-m-3), Note 1, Page 89.

A Balk is Ignored When:

- The balk is a pitched ball and the batter hits the ball, causing both the batter and runners to advance one base.

  Result: The ball stays live.

  Rule 9: Section: 3-m-1), Page 89.

- The balk becomes a wild pitch that is either ball four or strike three, and the batter and all runners advance one base.

  Rule 9: Section: 3-m-1), Example, Page 89.

It is a Balk When:

- The pitcher, while in contact with the pitcher's plate, feints and does not complete the throw toward the batter, first base, or third base.

  Note: The step to third and throw to first base is no longer legal.

  Rule 9: Section: 3-a, Page 87.

- The pitcher, while in contact with the pitcher's plate, does not step directly toward the base, gaining ground, at which he is attempting to retire a runner or prevent a runner from advancing.

  Rule 9: Section: 3-c, Page 87.

- The pitcher's non-pivot foot does not step directly towards and gain ground to that base, while he throws or feints to either put out or drive back a runner.

  Rule 9: Section: 1-a-6, Page 83, 84.
  Rule 9: Section: 3-c-1, Page 88.

  1. Stepping without throwing to second while occupied or driving back a runner is legal.

  Rule 9: Section: 3-c-6, Page 88.

- The pitcher, while in contact with the pitcher's plate, drops the ball intentionally or unintentionally and the ball stays in fair ground with runners on base.

  Rule 9: Section: 2-b, Page 85.

  Exceptions:

  1. When the ball rolls foul it is not a balk, but instead the batter is awarded a ball.

     Rule 9: Section: 2-b-Penalty, Page 85.

  2. With no runners on, it is a no pitch.

     Rule 9: Section: 2-b-Penalty, Page 85.

- The pitcher's entire non-pivot foot or any part of the stride leg breaks the plane of the back edge of the pitcher's plate and he does not throw or feint a motion to second base, or pitch the batter.

  Result: The pitcher must either pitch to home plate or feint or throw to second base.

  Rule 9: Section: 3-l, Page 89.

- The pitcher fails to step ahead of a snap throw while attempting to pick off runner.

  Rule 9: Section: 3-c-3), Page 88.

- The pitcher begins his pitching motion while not in contact with the pitching rubber.

  Rule 9: Section: 3-m, Page 89.

- The pitcher stands with one or both feet on any part of the mound with runners on base while not in possession of the ball.

  Author's Note: This infraction often takes place while the defense is attempting a hidden ball trick.

  Rule 9: Section: 3-f, Page 88.

- The pitcher, from the set position, fails to come to a complete and discernible obvious stop or stops twice (double set).

  Rule 9: Section: 3-j, Page 88.

  Exception: With no baserunners, the pitcher does not need to come to a complete and discernible stop.

  Rule 9: Section: 3-j, Note, Page 88.

- The pitcher, after coming set, stops his delivery motion before releasing the ball.

Rule 9: Section: 3-g. Page 88.

Exception: When the batter steps out of the box and holds up his hand or any other actions that cause the pitcher to stop his motion, it is not a balk.

Rule 9: Section: 3-g, Note, Page 88.

- The pitcher, after bringing his hands together, separates his hands and fails to pitch or throw to a base.

Rule 9: Section: 3-h, Page 88.

Exception: The pitcher, prior to taking a legal pitching position, may briefly separate hands to adjust his grip on the ball.

Rule 9: Section: 3-h, Note, Page 88.

- From a windup position, the pitcher pumps more than twice before his delivery.

Rule 9: Section: 3-k, Page 88.

- The pitcher quick-pitches.

Rule 9: Section: 3-d, Page 88.

1. When a runner on third breaks for home, the pitcher can speed up his delivery, but must use a normal pitching sequence and arm action.

Rule 9: Section: 3-d, Note, Page 88.

- The catcher is not in the catcher's box with both feet prior to pitcher releasing pitch.

Rule 9: Section: 3-i, Page 88.

Exception: With no runners on, this is an illegal pitch.

Rule 9: Section: 3-i, Note, Page 88.

Penalty: A ball is awarded to the batter, unless the batter reaches base.

Rule 9: Section: 1-d, Page 85.

It is Not a Balk When:

- A coach or player uses unsportsmanlike tactics for the obvious purpose of making the pitcher commit a balk or disrupt the pitcher's delivery.

  Rule 5: Section: 15-a-2, Page 53.

  Note: When a balk, illegal pitch, or ball is called, the pitch will be nullified.

  Rule 5: Section: 15-a-2, Page 53.

  Result: The offender will be ejected and receive a one-game suspension.

  Rule 5: Section: 15-a-2, Penalty, Page 53.

- The pitcher throws to the first baseman, who is playing off the base and moving toward first base attempting to make a play on the runner.

  Rule 9: Section: 3-c-1), Note, Page 88.

It is a Pitching Violation When:

- The pitcher makes an illegal pitch or quick pitch when bases are unoccupied.

  Rule 9, Section: 2-a, Page 85.

  Penalty: Call the pitch a ball, unless the batter reaches first base.

  Rule 9: Section: 2-a, Penalty, Page 85.

- The pitcher, after going to his mouth with his fingers, fails to wipe off fingers before making contact with pitcher's plate.

  Rule 9: Section: 2-d, Page 85.

  Penalty: A ball is called with each violation.

  Rule 9: Section: 2-d, Penalty, Page 85.

- The pitcher goes to the mouth while in contact with the pitching plate.

  Rule 9: Section: 2-d, Note 1-P, Page 85.

  Penalty: Ball awarded to the batter.

  Rule 9: Section: 2-d, Note 1, Penalty, Page 85.

- The pitcher causes delay of game.

  Rule 9: Section: 2-c, Page 85.

  Penalty: After warning each pitcher, a ball is then called for each following violation.

  Rule 9: Section: 2-c, Penalty, Page 85.

Section Continued on Page 10

- The pitcher must be in contact with the pitcher's plate while taking signs from the catcher.

Rule 9: Section: 2-j, Page 87.

Penalty: A ball shall be called each time a pitcher violates this rule.

Rule 9: Section: 2-j, Penalty, Page 87.

Exception: The violation will be ignored when the pitcher pitches from this illegal position, the batter reaches first base, and no runner is put out before advancing at least one base.

Rule 9: Section: 2-j, Penalty, Page 87.

- The pitcher applies any foreign substance or moisture to the ball or his hands or defaces the ball.

Rule 9: Section: 2-e, Pages 85 – 86.

Penalty: First, warn the pitcher. On the second offense, eject.

Rule 9: Section: 2-e, Penalty, Pages 85 – 86.

- The pitcher, intentionally or unintentionally, drops the ball while in contact with the pitcher's plate with the bases unoccupied.

Rule 9: Section: 2-b, Page 85.

Penalties:

1. When the ball rolls foul, it is called a ball.
2. When the ball stays in fair territory, it is considered a no pitch.

Rule 9: Section: 2-b, Penalty, Page 85.

Author's Summary, Balk

- From the windup or set position, any movement associated with the delivery of the ball commits the pitcher to pitch without interruption.

  Rule 9: Section: 1-a, Page 84.
  Rule 9: Section: 1-b, Page 84.

- The pitcher, in the windup or set position, after bringing his hands together, can only separate them in order to:

  1. Pitch.

     Rule 9: Section: 1-a-1)-a), Page 83.
     Rule 9: Section: 3-h, Page 88

  2. Make a legal attempt to pick off or drive back a runner.

     Rule 9: Section: 1-a-1)-b), Page 83.
     Rule 9: Section: 1-b, Page 83.
     Rule 9: Section: 3-h, Page 88.

  3. Legally disengage pivot foot from pitcher's plate.

     Rule 9: Section: 1-a-1)-c), Page 83.
     Rule 9: Section: 1-c, Page 85.

- When a balk is delivered to the batter, and the batter and all runners advance at least one base, the balk is ignored.

  Result: The ball remains in play.

  Rule 9: Section: 3-m-1, Page 89.

- A jump turn is legal, but the lead foot must gain distance and direction to the base in which the throw is made.

  Rule 9: Section: 3-c-5, Page 88.

- For the pitcher to legally disengage the pitcher's plate, he must step backward off the pitcher's plate with his pivot foot first before moving his free foot.

  Rule 9: Section: 1-e, Note, Page 85.

- When the pitcher legally disengages the pitcher's plate, he becomes a fielder. Restrictions as a pitcher no longer apply.

Rule 9: Section: 1-e, Page 85.

Hidden Ball Trick

- The basics:
    1. An infielder keeps the live ball hidden from sight.
    2. Baserunner assume the pitcher has the ball and steps off the base.
    3. Defensive player with the ball tags runner off the base, for the out.
- The deception:
    1. The play is obviously designed to "trick" the runners, but more importantly it can trick umpires as well. This play is a perfect example of why umpires should never take their eyes off a live ball.
- The ruling:
    1. For a hidden ball trick to be legal (not a balk), the pitcher cannot stand on any part of the mound without the ball. Otherwise it is a balk.

Rule 9: Section: 3-f, Page 88.

- Things you must know:
    1. Who has the ball?
    2. The pitcher's location to determine when it's a potential out or a balk.
    3. The base umpire should be focused on the ball and an impending tag; the plate umpire should be focused on the pitcher's location.
    4. A balk supersedes the hidden-ball-trick out and baserunners are awarded one base.

Rule 9: Section: 3-f, Page 88.

Base Running Awards and Appeals

When an infraction or a batted or thrown ball goes out of play, what are the appropriate base award to give to the base runners? Rulings are listed under one base, two base, and three base awards in order to connect similar infractions with similar awards. We have also included base awards for interference and obstruction, because when these two infractions happen it's often extremely chaotic on the field. Being able to quickly apply the appropriate base award is an effective way to defuse problems.

One Base Award When:

- A pitcher's pitch or a throw (pickoff attempt) while in contact with pitcher's plate and one of the following three actions happen:
  1. Ball goes into a dead ball area.
  2. Ball is intentionally touched by a spectator.
  3. Ball lodges in umpire's or catcher's clothing or equipment.

  Award: All runners are awarded one base.

  Rule 8: Section: 3-k, Page 74.

- The umpire awards four balls to the batter.

  Rule 8: Section: 2-b, Page 71.

- A fielder catches a batted ball then jumps or falls over or through a fence while retaining the ball.

  Result: The batter is out and all runners advance one base.

  Rule 8: Section: 3-m, Page 74.

- A fielder, after making a legal catch, steps into a bench, dugout, or dead-ball area.

  Result: The ball is dead and runners are awarded one base.

  Rule 6: Section: 1-d, Page 57.

- A batter is hit by a pitched ball that he is not attempting to strike.

  Result: The ball is immediately dead and the batter is awarded first base.

  Rule 8: Section: 2-d, Page 71.

Ruling Continued on Page 17

Clarification: A batter may not move to intentionally get hit by the pitch, regardless of the location of the pitch. A batter must avoid being hit whenever possible, unless the pitch is in the batter's box.

Rule 8: Section: 2-d-1), Page 71.

Example: When the ball is within the batter's box occupied by the batter and the batter makes no movement to intentionally get hit by the pitch, the batter is awarded first base. When the batter freezes inside the batter's box and is hit by the pitch, he is awarded first base.

Rule 8: Section: 2-d-1)-b), Pages 71 – 72.

- The ball is in the strike zone when it touches the batter, the batter moved to intentionally get hit, or the batter freezes to allow the pitch that is not within the batter's box to hit him.

Result: The ball is dead and is called a strike; the batter is not awarded first base.

Rule 8: Section: 2-d-1)-b), Page 71 – 72.

- Any defensive player (usually the catcher) interferes with the batter's swing or prevents the batter from striking the ball.

Rule 8: Section: 2-e, Page 72.

Results:

1. It is a delayed dead ball; let the play finish.

Rule 8: Section: 2-e-1, Page 72.

- When play continues after the interference, the offense can ignore the interference and accept the outcomes of the play.

Rule 8: Section: 2-e, Page 72.

Section Continued on Page 18

1. When all other runners advance one base and the batter reaches first base, the interference is ignored.

   Rule 8: Section: 2-e-1, Page 72.

2. When baserunners are attempting to steal during the interference, runners will be awarded the base they were stealing

   Rule 8: Section: 2-e-2, Page 72.

3. When runners are not attempting to steal during a catcher's interference with the batter's swing, the runners will only advance when forced.

   Rule 8: Section: 2-e-2, Page 72.

Two Base Award When:

- The first throw by infielder goes out of play, and the throw is not from a pitcher in contact with the pitcher's plate.

  Rule 8: Section: 3-o-3), Note 1, Page 75.

  Results:

  1. It is an immediate dead ball.

     Rule 8: Section: 3-o-3), Page 75.

  2. Batter-runner and runners are awarded two bases.

     Rule 8: Section: 3-o, Page 74.

  3. Bases are awarded from the runner's location at the time of pitch.

     Rule 8: Section: 3-o-3), Note 1, Page 75.

     Exceptions:

     a. When a pitcher, while in contact with the pitcher's plate, throws the ball out of play, it is a one base award.

        Rule 8, Section: 3-3), Page 75.

     b. When on the first play all runners, including the batter-runner, advanced one base before the baseball was thrown or released out of play, base awards would then be from the runner's location at the time of throw.

        Rule 8: Section: 3-o-3), Note 1, Exception, Page 75

Section Continued on Page 20.

- The second play by an infielder goes out of play.

  Results:

  1. It is an immediate dead ball.

     Rule 8: Section: 3-3), Page 75.

  2. Bases are awarded from the runner's location at the time of throw.

     No ruling provided in the NCAA Rule Book.

- Any throw by an outfielder goes out of play.

  Rule 8: Section: 3-o-3), Note 1, Page 75.

  Results:

  1. It is an immediate dead ball.

     Rule 8: Section: 3-3), Page 75.

  2. Batter-runner and runners are awarded two bases from their location at the time of throw.

     Rule 8: Section: 3-o, Page 74.
     Rule 8: Section: 3-3), Note 1, Page 75.

- A fielder intentionally deflects, throws, kicks, or carries the ball into dead-ball territory.

  Result: Runners are awarded two bases from the time of illegal act.

  Rule 8: Section: 3-o-5, Page 75.

- A fair ball is intentionally touched by any of the fielder's detached equipment, bases are awarded from the time of illegal act.

  Rule 8: Section: 3-g, Page 74.

  Results:

  1. This is a delayed dead ball and runners may advance at their own risk.

     Rule 8: Section: 3-g-4), Page 74.
  2. When the ball is thrown, batter-runner and runners are awarded two bases from the time of illegal act.

     Rule 8: Section: 3-g-2), Page 74.
  3. When it is a batted fair ball or foul ball with a chance of becoming fair, the award is three bases from the time of illegal act.

     Rule 8: Section: 3-g-1), Page 74.

Three Base Award When:

- A fair or foul-batted ball that has a chance of becoming fair is touched by a fielder's detached equipment, bases are awarded from the time of illegal act.

  Rule 8: Section: 3-g-1), Page 74.

  1. This is a delayed dead ball and runners may advance further at their own risk.

     Rule 8: Section: 3-g-4), Page 74.

Award: The runners are awarded three bases.

Rule 8: Section: 3-g-1, Page 74.

Defensive Catcher's Interference Rulings

- When the catcher interferes on a squeeze play, the following happens:
  1. The umpire calls it a balk.
  2. The batter is awarded first base
  3. The run scores.
  4. All runners advance one base on the balk created by catcher's interference.

Rule 8: Section: 3-p, Page 75.
Rule 8: Section: 2-e, Exception, Page 72.

- When the batter's swing, while loosening up and preparing for a pitch, hits the catcher or his glove, it is not catcher's interference and the following will happen:
  1. The umpire immediately calls time.
  2. Neither a pitch nor swing will be allowed.

Rule 8: Section: 2-e, Note, Page 72.

Base Awards for Interference Rulings

- When a batter, batter-runner, or baserunner is called out for interference, all other runners return to the bases last touched at the time of interference.

  Rule 2: Section: 51, Note 1, Page 29.

- When the batter-runner does not reach first base at the time of the interference, all runners return to the bases at the time of the pitch.

  Rule 2: Section: 51, Note 2, Page 29.

- When there is an intervening play made on another runner, all runners return to the bases last touched at the time of interference.

  Rule 2: Section: 51, Note 2, Page 29.

Base Awards for Obstruction Rulings

- Type One Obstruction is against a runner on whom a play is being made.

  Example: A pick off play when the defensive player is blocking the base without clear possession of the ball.

  Rule 8: Section: 3-e-1), Penalty Note, Page 73.

  Results:

  1. It is an immediate dead ball
  2. The umpire calls time and says "That's obstruction."
  3. The runner being played on will be awarded one base beyond the last base he had reached.
  4. All runners will be awarded bases they would have reached had there been no obstruction.

  Rule 2: Section: 55, Page 30.
  Rule 8, Section: 3-e-1), Penalty Note, Page 73.

- Type Two Obstruction against a runner on whom a play is not being made.

  Results:

  1. The umpire points and loudly calls "That's obstruction," and will let the play continue
  2. When all action and play has topped, the umpire will call time and impose any penalties that would nullify the act of obstruction.

  Rule 8: Section: 3-2, Penalty, Page 73.

  Note: Umpires may confer to discuss reasonable base awards if the obstruction had not occurred.

  Rule 8: Section: 3-2, Note, Page 73.

Baserunner Appeal / Squeeze Play / Catch and Carry

Base running appeals have specific protocol in order for the appeal to be legal, and if the specific protocol is not followed, the appeal is not upheld. Appeals can also impact whether or not a run is scored after a third out is made. Thcsc are just few of the many reasons for understanding exactly what an appeal ruling is stating. Squeeze plays happen extremely quickly with lots of extremely complicated moving parts to watch, culminating often with large bodies colliding at the plate. A solid understanding of these rulings is great to have. The same is true for catch and carry rulings. While less explosive, they are just as important.

Definition of an Appeal

- A player or coach stating the opposing team violated a rule or the umpires misinterpreted a rule or any act that clearly indicates an appeal.

Rule 2: Section: 2, Page 21.

Author's examples of specific appeals: Batting out of order, check swing, runner on a fly ball leaving his base before the ball is touched, or runner missing a base.

Legal Baserunner Appeal Rulings

- A live ball baserunner appeal is legal.

  Rule 8: Section: 6-b-1)-a), Page 80.

- For a baserunner appeal to be legal, the appeal must be made before anyone of these three things happen:
  1. The first legal or illegal pitch is made to the next batter.
  2. A play or attempted play is made.
  3. Before the pitcher and all infielders leave fair territory on their way to the dugout, when it is the end of an inning or game ending appeal.

  Rule 8: Section: 6-b, Page 80.
  Rule 8: Section: 6-b-8), Page 80.

- The defensive team still has the right to appeal when the offensive team initiates a play before the next pitch.

  Rule 8: Section: 6-b-4), Page 80.

- An appeal is not considered a play or attempted play.

  Exception: An appeal is considered a play when the pitcher balks during the appeal.

  Rule 8: Section: 6-b-2), Page 80.

Section Continued on Page 30

- In order for a dead ball appeal to be legal, the following must happen:
  1. The pitcher must receive the ball from the umpire and hold the ball while in contact with the rubber.

     Rule 8: Section: 6-b-1)-b), Page 80.
  2. When the umpire puts the ball into play, the pitcher must legally disengage the pitching rubber, then throw to the base where a tag can be applied to either the runner or base.

     Rule 8: Section: 6-b-1)-b), Page 80.
  3. All defensive players, except the catcher must be in fair ground. A defensive player may go into foul ground to back up a throw on the appeal

     Rule 5: Section: 4-c, Penalty, Page 46.
- When the umpire unintentionally puts the ball in play while a defensive player other than the catcher is in foul ground, the defense is still eligible to make a legal appeal on the same runner once the ball is then legally put in play.

  Rule 5: Section: 4-c, Penalty, Page 46.

The Runner is Out on Appeal When:

- A fielder tags the runner or the base before the baserunner can retouch the base, after a fair or foul fly ball is touched by a fielder making a legal catch.

  Rule 8: Section: 6-1), Page 79.

- The runner, in an effort to get a running start, begins from a position behind the base during either a tag up or pitch.

  Rule 8: Section: 6-2), Page 79.

- The runner, who is either advancing or retuning, fails to touch each base. Either the runner or the missed base may be tagged for the out.

  Rule 8: Section: 6-3), Page 79.

- No runner may return to touch a missed base after the following runner has scored.

  Rule 8: Section: 6-3), Note 1, Page 80.

- Once a ball becomes dead, no runner may return to touch a missed base or the one he just left when the runner has advanced to and touched a base beyond the missed base.

  Rule 8: Section: 6-3), Note 2, Page 80.

- After a fly ball is caught and the ball is thrown out of play while the runner is attempting to return to his original base, the runner may retouch, and the base award for the ball going out of play is made from his original base.

  Rule 8: Section: 6-3), Note 3 Page 80.

- When a runner misses a base due to obstruction, the runner is not called out on appeal for missing the base.

  Rule 8: Section: 6-3), Note 4 Page 80.

Catch and Carry Rulings

- When a fielder makes a legal catch on a fly ball, then:
    1. Jumps over or through a fence.
    2. Falls over or through a fence.

    Results:

    a. It is an immediate dead ball.

    b. The batter is out.

    c. All runners are awarded one base.

Rule 8: Section: 3-m, Page 74.

Rule 6: Section: 1-d, Page 57.

Squeeze Play with Catcher's Interference Rulings

- On an attempted squeeze play or steal of home plate, it is catcher's interference when the catcher, without the ball, steps on or in front of home plate or touches the batter or bat. It is a balk on the pitcher.

Rule 8: Section: 3-p, Page 75.

Results:

1. It is an immediate dead ball.
2. The batter is awarded first base on the interference.
3. The run scores.
4. It is a balk, all baserunners advance one base.

Rule 8: Section: 3-p, Penalty, Page 75.

Batting Out of Order

For years as an umpire, I found the rule language in official rule books about batting out of order impossible to understand. We have changed that and provided content regarding batting out of order that is reader friendly and easily retained. We have also created examples of batting out of order scenarios that can and do happen to define and illustrate the infraction and the correct ruling that would apply. We have been able to create content that is no longer complicated or confusing, but rather straightforward and undemanding. No matter how screwed up the batting order gets, you will now know what to do.

Legal Appeal for Batting Out of Order

- For a batting out of order appeal to be legal, the appeal must be made before these two things happen:
    1. The first pitch is made to the next batter of either team.
    2. A play or attempted play is made.

Rule 7: Section: 11-a-2), Page 68.

Batting Out of Order Rulings

- When an improper batter is discovered before completing his turn at bat, the proper batter replaces the improper batter and assume the improper batter's pitch count.
  Rule 7: Section: 11-a-1), Page 68.
- During an improper batter's at bat, any baserunner advances are considered legal.
  Rule 7: Section: 11-a-2), Page 68.
- After an improper batter completes his at-bat and is put out or becomes a baserunner and a legal appeal is made, the proper batter who should have batted is called out.

  Result: All runners return to bases occupied before the last action that caused the improper batter to become a batter-runner.

  Rule 7: Section: 11-a-2), Page 68.
- On a legal appeal wherein the proper batter is called out for not batting in his correct spot, the next legal batter is whoever follows the proper batter who was called out in the order.

  Rule 7: Section: 11-a-2), Page 68.
- When an improper batter completes his at bat and there is either no appeal or an illegal appeal, that improper batter then becomes the newly legalized proper batter.
  Rule 7: Section: 11-a-3), Page 68.
- When there is no legal appeal and the improper batter becomes the newly legalized proper batter, the legal batting order would then continue with whoever follows that newly legalized proper batter as listed in the batting order.
  Rule 7: Section: 11-a-4), Page 68.

- When an improper batter becomes legal and is on base and their legal turn at bat arrives, they are skipped over and the batter who follows him bats.

Rule 7: Section: 11-a-5), Page 68.

Author's Examples for Batting Out of Order

- Example 1: The official lineup card reads the three-spot batter should be batting, but instead the four-spot batter is up at bat and has a pitch count of one ball, two strikes. Before the four-spot batter completes his at bat, the offense or defense can and does appeal the umpire.

  Result: The illegal four-spot batter did not complete his at bat, the proper three-spot batter who should be batting would then replace the illegal four-spot batter and assumes the improper batter's pitch count.

  Rule 7: Section: 11-a-1), Page 68.

- Example 2: The four-spot batter gets a base hit, but, on a legal appeal, is discovered that he batted out of order. The three-spot batter should have batted.

  Result: The proper three spot batter is called out for failing to bat in his correct spot in the line-up. The illegal four spot who just batted, would then return to bat in his legal batting spot following the three-spot batter.

  Rule 7: Section: 11-a-2), Page 68.

- Example 3: The four-spot batter bats out of order ahead of the three-spot batter, and the four-spot batter gets a base hit. The three-spot batter then comes up to bat and a strike is thrown, then an appeal is made.

  Result: Because a pitch was thrown, the appeal is denied and the four-spot batter becomes the newly legalized proper batter. Because the four-spot batter has become the last legal player to bat, the five-spot batter would replace the three-spot batter at bat and assumes the three-spot's pitch count.

  Rule 7: Section: 11-a-3), Page 68.
  Rule 7: Section: 11-a-4), Page 68.

- Example 4: The four-spot batter bats out of order ahead of the three-spot batter and gets thrown out at first base. The three-spot batter comes to the plate and a pitch is thrown, then an appeal is made.

  Result: Even though the four-spot batter was thrown out, there was no appeal and a pitch was thrown, which now makes the four-spot batter the last legal proper batter. His time at bat becomes official. The five-spot batter would then take the three-spot batter's place at bat and assume his pitch count.

  Rule 7: Section: 11-a-3), Page 68.
  Rule 7: Section: 11-a-4), Page 68.

  Author's Note: No matter how badly the batting order becomes, legal or illegal appeal or still at bat, it can easily be corrected as in the following examples.

- Example 5: The eight-spot batter is batting in the three-spot batter's position in the batting order.

  Variations and Results:

  1. The eight-spot batter is discovered while still at bat.

     Result: The three-spot batter would replace the eight-spot batter at bat and assume the eight-spot batter's pitch count.

     Rule 7: Section: 11-a-1), Page 68.

  2. After the eight-spot batter reaches base but before another pitch is made, a legal appeal is made.

     Result: The three-spot batter is called out for failing to bat in his correct spot and the four-spot batter would become the next proper batter.

     Rule 7: Section: 11-a-2), Page 68.

3. After the eight-spot batter reaches base, an illegal appeal or no appeal takes place.

   Result: Because the eight-spot batter has become the newly legalized proper batter, the nine-spot batter would be the next proper batter.

   Rule 7: Section: 11-a-3), Page 68.
   Rule 7: Section: 11-a-4), Page 68.

Author's Note: Because the three-spot batter failed to bat in his correct spot, and the eight-spot batter became the new legalized proper batter, batters in the four through seven spots lose the opportunity to bat.

Rule 7: Section: 11-a-4), Page 68.

1. The eight-spot batter gets thrown out at first base. The three-spot batter comes to the plate, and a pitch is thrown, then an appeal is made.

   Even though the eight-spot batter was thrown out, there was no appeal, and a pitch was thrown. Which now makes the eight-spot batter the last legal proper batter, and his time at bat becomes official. The nine-spot batter would then take the three-spot batter's place at bat and assume his pitch count.

   Rule 7: Section: 11-a-3), Page 68.
   Rule 7: Section: 11-a-4), Page 68.

Author's Summary for Batting Out of Order

- The next proper batter is always be whoever follows either the last proper batter or the newly legalized proper batter.

Rule 7: Section: 11-a-4), Page 68.

Catch

A simple as it may seem, the definition of a catch in bascball, and how it is written in official baseball rule books, turns what should be a simple matter into confusion and uncertainty. When a fielder gets a fly ball in his glove and travels several more steps and the ball falls to the ground, making a definitive ruling that is cloudy in your own mind is a recipe for disaster. We convert confusion and uncertainty into definitive clear basic English. So, when you make a ruling on the field, it is acquired from easily retained information that can be easily articulated to questioning players and coaches.

Definition of a Catch

- A ball in flight is in secure possession of a fielder's hand or glove while firmly holding it.

  Rule 2: Section: 16, Page 22.

- The fielder cannot use any article of clothing, protective equipment, or any part of his uniform to secure the ball.

  Rule 2: Section: 16, Page 22.

- A catch is valid when the fielder demonstrates the following:

  1. Complete control of the ball.
  2. The release of the ball is voluntary and intentional.

  Rule 2: Section: 16, Page 22.

- Two situations can determine a voluntary and intentional release:

  1. When the momentum of the catch is complete.

     Example: The fielder is now running in a different direction, while still in secure possession of the ball.

     Rule 2: Section: 16-1), Page 22.

  2. When the fielder is reaching for the ball to make a throw.

     Rule 2: Section: 16-2), Page 22.

     Example: When the runner has the ball securely held in his glove and while reaching for the ball or while making a throw, it falls to the ground, it is still considered a legal catch.

     Rule 2: Section: 16-2)-c, Page 22.

Definition of No Catch

- When the fielder collides with another player or the fence or falls down and, immediately after or at the same time, the fielder drops the ball, it is not a catch.

  Rule 2: Section: 16-2)-a, Page 22.

- When any fly ball is touched by a defensive player and then hits an offensive player or umpire and is then caught again by any defensive player, it is not a catch.

  Rule 2: Section: 16-2)-b, Page 22.

- When either foot of the defensive player is touching dead-ball territory, it is not a catch.

  Rule 2: Section: 16-2)-d, Page 22.

Changing a Catch to a No Catch

- When changing an outfield or foul fly ball from a catch to a no catch, the following can happen:
    1. Umpires can conference on any fair-batted fly ball hit into the outfield or for any foul fly ball to get more information to establish if a catch was made or if it was not a catch.

        Appendix E: Section: 1-C-9, Page 109.

    2. Umpires can change a catch call to a no catch, and the following rulings apply:

        Appendix E: Section: 1-C-9, Page 109.

        a. The ball is dead.

        Appendix E: Section: 1-C-9-a), Page 109.

        b. The batter goes to first base.

        Appendix E: Section: 1-C-9-b), Page 109.

        c. The baserunners advance one base from the base they occupied at the time of the pitch.

        Appendix E: Section: 1-C-9-c, Page 109.

    3. For the purpose of this rule, once a batted fly ball passes the nearest infielder, it is considered hit into the outfield. These rulings do not apply to a line drive hit to an infielder.

        Appendix E: Section: 1-C-10, Note 2, Page 109.

- These rulings do not apply to a line drive hit to an infielder.

    Appendix E: Section: 1-C-10-Note 2, Page 109.

Changing a No Catch to a Catch

- When changing an outfield or foul fly ball from a No Catch to a Catch, the following can happen:

    1. Umpires can conference after any fair-batted fly ball hit into the outfield or for any foul fly ball in order to get more information to establish if a catch was made or if it was not a catch.

        Appendix E: Section: 1-C-10, Page 109.

    2. Umpires can change a no catch call to a catch, and the following rulings apply:

        a. The ball is dead.

        Appendix E: Section: 1-C-10-a), Page 109.

        b. All actions prior to the ball becoming dead are invalid.

        Appendix E: Section: 1-C-10-b), Page 109.

        c. The batter is out on the catch.

        Appendix E: Section: 1-C-10-c), Page 109.

        d. Baserunners return to the base occupied at the time of the pitch.

        Appendix E: Section: 1-C-10-d), Page 109.

    3. For the purpose of this rule, once a batted fly ball passes the nearest infielder, it is considered hit into the outfield. These rulings do not apply to a line drive hit to an infielder.

        Appendix E: Section: 1-C-10, Note 2, Page 109.

Changing an Infield, Fly Ball No Catch to a Catch

- You can change an infield fly ball from a no catch to a catch when:
    1. Runners are on base and the catch results in a third out.
    2. There are no runners on base.

Appendix E: Section: 1-C-10, Note 1, Page 109.

Intentionally Dropped Fly Ball

- When an in fielder intentionally drops a batted or bunted fair fly ball or line drive with less than two outs with runners on any bases,
    1. The ball is immediately dead.
    2. The batter is out.
    3. All runners return to their original bases.

  Rule 7: Section: 11-q, Page 70.

- When the ball drops untouched to the ground,
    1. The batter is not out.

       Exception: When an infield fly rule is in effect, the batter is out.
    2. The ball stays live.
    3. Runners may advance at their own risk.

  Rule 7: Section: 11-q, Note, Page 70.

Conferences

How many charged conferences before the pitcher gets pulled in regulation play? How many charged conferences before a pitcher gets pulled in extra innings? If I don't use my charged conferences in regulation play, can I use them in extra innings? When do conference end? Easy enough simple questions with the answers collected, converted into basic English, and organized into an easy-to-find format.

Offense Conference Rulings

- Each team is allowed three regular-inning offensive conferences plus one extra-inning offensive conference.

  Rule 6: Section: 5-f, Page 60.

  1. Unused offense conferences carry over from regulation. They are added to the one extra-inning conference.

     Rule 6: Section: 5-f-3), Page 60.

- All offensive conferences can be used in the same inning.

  Rule 6: Section: 5-f, Note, Page 60.

- An offensive conference shall not be charged during a defensive team's timeout for a pitching change.
  1. In order for Batters or runners to leave their positions during a charged defensive conference they must request an offensive charged conference.

     Rule 6: Section: 5-f-4), Page 60.

  2. When runners do not return to their bases prior to the last warm-up pitch, they are at risk of being charged a offensive conference.

     Rule 6: Section: 5-f 4), Page 60.

- Umpires record and notify offensive coaches of their charged conferences.

  Rule 6: Section: 5-f-1), Page 60.

- Umpires record and advise offensive coaches when they have used all their allowed charged conferences before penalizing.

Rule 6: Section: 5-f-2), Page 60.

Penalties:

1. When a player is involved in the illegal charged offensive conference, he is removed from the game.
2. When the illegal meeting is between the head coach and an assistant coach, the assistant coach is removed from the game.

Rule 6: Section: 5-f -2, Penalty, Page 60.

Defense Conference Rulings

- A team is allowed six defensive conferences during a regulation game, but only three of these conferences may include a coach.

  Note: This 2019 – 20 rule change is intended to set a limit for the number of conferences initiated by defensive players.

  Rule 6: Section: 5-f, Page 60.

- A coach is allowed three free trips to the mound in a game, plus one free trip to the mound in extra innings.

  Rule 9: Section: 4-a, Page 89.

  1. It is considered a free trip when a coach goes to the mound and does not remove the pitcher.

  Rule 9: Section: 4-a-1), Page 89.

- When a coach has a defensive conference to speak with any defensive player, whether the player goes to the mound or not. It is considered a charged conference.

  Rule 9: Section: 4-a-3), Page 90.

- A pitcher must be removed for the remainder of the game when:

  1. A coach or any of the team non-playing staff makes a second trip to the mound in the same inning to talk with same pitcher.
  2. As soon as the coach crosses the foul line approaching the mound, he will notify an umpire who the relief pitcher is.

  Rule 9: Section: 4-b, Page 90.

- A coach cannot take a second trip to the mound in the same inning with the same batter at bat.

  Exception: A second trip is allowed when a pinch hitter enters the game, but the pitcher must still be removed.

  Rule 9: Section: 4-c, Page 90.

- Umpires are to warn coaches that they are not to go to the mound a second time in the same inning with the same batter.

  Penalty: When the coach continues to the mound after a warning, he is ejected, and the pitcher completes pitching to the batter. Then after that batter has complete his at-bat, the pitcher must be removed.

  Rule 9: Section: 4-c-3), Page 91.

- If a coach has mistakenly been granted a fourth visit to the mound for a conference, the pitcher is removed after the batter complete the at-bat.

  1. The removed pitcher cannot re-enter as pitcher.

  Rule 9: Section: 4-c-2), Page 90 – 91.

- When there is a lengthy offensive injury timeout, the defensive coach and pitcher can confer without being penalized a charged conference.

  1. When the defensive visit delays play past the injury time out, a charged conference is given to the defense.

  Rule 9: Section: 4-a-6, Page 90.

Pitchers Should be Removed When:

- Coach uses all of his three free trips, then has a fourth conference.

  Rule 9: Section: 4-a-1), Page 89.

- Coach goes to the mound twice in the same inning with the same pitcher.

  Rule 9: Section: 4-b, Page 90.

- The coach, after having one visit to the mound in same inning with same pitcher or has used his three free trips, announces a pitching change to the plate umpire but does not go to the mound. This is still recorded as a conference.

  Note: When the pitcher is moved to a defensive position, he cannot return to pitch.

  Rule 9: Section: 4-b, Note 1, Page 90.

Defense Conference Begins and Ends When:

- The defensive-charged conference begins when the coach crosses the foul line.

  Rule 9: Section: 4-d, Page 91.

- The defensive-charged conference ends when the coach:

  1. Leaves the dirt circle.
  2. Pitcher begins his warm up pitches.

  Rule 9: Section: 4-d, Page 91.

Extra-Inning Offense & Defense Conferences

- In extra innings, both offense and defense are awarded one additional conference.

Rule 6: Section: 5-f, Page 60.

1. Both the offense's and defense's unused regulation conferences carry over and are added to the extra inning conferences.

Rule 6: Section: 5-f-3, Page 62.
Rule 9: Section: 4-a-4, Page 90.

Designated Hitter & P/Dh

We did extensive work to produce this chapter in an effort to collect, organize, and structure rulings in manner so that you the reader can study, understand, retain, and apply this complicated topic when needed. We have collected and listed rulings together for the ten-player designated hitter and the nine-player P/DH. We have listed three ways a nine-player P/DH lineup can become a ten-player lineup. We have also listed when both the nine-player P/DH and a ten-player designated hitter are terminated. This does effectively what no other rule book is able to do when attempting to teach this rule topic.

Nine-Player Lineup, P/DH Rulings

- When the pitcher is listed batting in a nine-player lineup, the pitcher is automatically considered both the pitcher and designated hitter (aka the P/DH).

  Rule 7: Section: 2-c, Page 63.

- The P/DH can be substituted for as either the pitcher or the designated hitter.

  Rule 7: Section: 2-c, Page 63.

- When the P/DH is moved to a defensive position, the DH is no long P/DH, but while at his new defensive position, he must bat in his original P/DH batting spot.

  Rule 7: Section: 2-e-2)-b), Page 65.

  1. The new pitcher must bat in the spot of the replaced defensive player.

     Rule 7: Section: 2-e-2)-c), Page 65.

- Once the P/DH goes to a defensive position, that defensive player may return as a pitcher once.

  Exception: When the P/DH pitcher, on a second trip in an inning or after the third free trip, that pitcher, once removed from the lineup, cannot return to pitch.

  Rule 7: Section: 2-e-2)-d), Page 65.

- When the P/DH is replaced offensively as the DH, the individual may remain as pitcher.

  Rule 7: Section: 2-e-3)-a), Page 65.

  1. After the P/DH is replaced as DH and remains as pitcher, he cannot move to a defensive position.

     Rule 7: Section: 2-e-3)-a)-(1), Page 65.

  2. After the P/DH is replaced as DH and remains as pitcher, he cannot return as DH.

     Rule 7: Section: 2-e-3)-a)-(2), Page 65.

- When the P/DH is ejected, he may be replaced by either one player continuing in nine-player lineup with a P/DH or ten-player lineup with two players, a non-batting pitcher, and a DH.

Rule 7: Section: 2-e-4)-a), Page 65.

Three Ways a Nine-Player Lineup Becomes a Ten-Player Lineup

1. A ten-player lineup can be created if the P/DH remains as pitcher with a new designated hitter. The following would happen:

   a. When the old P/DH remains as a pitcher, and a new player becomes the DH, the pitcher would be listed in the non-batting tenth spot in the newly created ten-player lineup.

   Rule 7: Section: 2-e-3)-a), Page 65.

   b. The new designated hitter would then bat in the old P/DH spot.

   Rule 7: Section: 2-b-1), Page 63.

   c. The replaced P/DH batter cannot move to another defensive position. He can only stay as pitcher.

   Rule 7: Section: 2-e-3)-a)-(1), Page 65.

   d. The replaced P/DH batter going into the ten-spot cannot return offensively to bat.

   Rule 7: Section: 2-e-3)-a)-(2), Page 65.

2. A ten-player lineup is created if the P/DH remains only as a designated hitter while being replaced by a new pitcher.

   Rule 7: Section: 2-e-1)-a)-(1), Page 65.

   a. New pitcher, becomes the tenth player in the non-batting spot, creating a new ten man line up.

      Rule 7: Section: 2-b-1), Page 63.

   b. Remaining as the DH, he can only bat in his original P/DH batting spot.

      Rule 7: Section: 2-b-1), Page 65.
      Rule 7: Section: 2-e-1)-a)-(1), Page 63.

   c. The DH, and any player who replaces the DH, cannot play any other positions or roles.

      Rule 7: Section: 2-e-1)-a)-(1), Page 63.

3. When the P/DH is ejected, the coach can switch to a ten-player lineup with a designated hitter and a non-batting pitcher listed in the tenth spot, or continue as a P/DH in a ten-man lineup.

   Rule 7: Section: 2-e-4)-a), Page 65.

Nine-Player Lineup, DH is Terminated When:

- The P/DH is moved to a defensive position.

  Rule 7: Section: 2-e-2), Page 65.

- The DH is terminated for the remainder of the game.

  Rule 7: Section: 2-e-2)-a), Page 65.

  1. The P/DH being placed at a defensive position must bat in the original spot in the batting order.

     Rule 7: Section: 2-e-2)-b), Page 65.

  2. The new pitcher bats in the replaced defensive player's spot.

     Rule 7: Section: 2-e-2-c, Page 65.

- A defensive player becomes the pitcher, replacing the P/DH.

  Rule 7: Section: 2-e-5, Page 65.

  1. The DH is terminated for the remainder of the game.

     Rule 7: Section: 2-e-5-a), Page 65.

  2. The (former) P/DH can assume the defensive player's position.

     Rule 7: Section: 2-e-5-b), Page 65.

  3. Any substitute player replacing the (former P/DH must bat in the same (former) P/DH spot in the batting order.

     Rule 7: Section: 2-e-5-c), Page 65.

Ten-Player Lineup, DH Rulings

- The DH can only bat for a starting pitcher and all following pitchers.

  Rule 7: Section: 2-a, Page 63.

- The DH may bat in any spot in the batting order, but the initial DH batting spot listed cannot be changed.

  Rule 7: Section: 2-b-1), Page 63.

- The DH must be listed on the ten-player lineup card and presented to the plate UIC before the game.

  Rule 7: Section: 2-b-2), Page 63.

  1. When a team uses a ten-player line-up, the pitcher is not listed in the one through nine batting order, the pitcher would be listed in the non-batting ten-spot.

     Rule 7: Section: 2-d-2, Page 63.

- A replaced DH player cannot return offensively.

  Rule 7: Section: 2-d-3)-a)-(1), Page 64.

- When the DH is ejected, the DH spot is not terminated and can be replaced with another player.

  Rule 7: Section: 2-d-9)-a), Page 65.

  1. The pitcher may become the P/DH, the all nine-player lineup rules shall apply from that point forward.

     Rule 7: Section: 2-d-9-b), Page 65.

- When a DH becomes the pitcher moved to the ten-spot, then later is pulled as pitcher, the following can happen:

  1. He can return to the batting order as the DH.

     Rule 7: Section: 2-d-6)-a), Page 64.

  2. DH is not terminated.

     Rule 7: Section: 2-d-6)-b), Page 64.

- A pitcher being replaced can be inserted into the DH spot if the coach immediately tells the plate umpire at the time of the substitution.

  Rule 7: Section: 2-d-1)-c), Page 63.

- The DH bats for new pitchers, the replaced pitcher cannot re-enter the game in any position or role. The replaced pitcher may not re-enter the game in any other capacity.

  Rule 7: Section: 2-d-1)-b), Page 63.

- When a DH player enters a defensive position, it terminates the DH, and the former DH must bat (stay) in his original DH spot.

  Rule 7: Section: 2-d-5)-b), Page 64.
  Rule 5: Section: 5-d, Page 46.

  Results:

  1. The pitcher will bat in the removed defensive player's batting spot.

     Rule 5: Section: 5-d, Page 46.

  2. When the DH is terminated, all nine-player lineup rules apply from this point forward.

     Rule 7: Section: 2-d-5)-a), Page 64.

Ten-Man DH is Terminated When:

- A pinch hitter bats for any player and then enters the game to pitch.

  Result: The DH's role is terminated for the remainder of the game.

  Rule 7: Section: 2-d-1)-e), Page 63.

- A DH enters the game as a defensive player.
  1. All nine-player lineup rules apply from this point forward.

  Rule 7: Section: 2-d-5-a), Page 64.

- A pitcher is moved to defensive position.

  Rule 7: Section: 2-d-2)-a), Page 63 – 64.

  Results:
  1. The pitcher entering a defensive position must bat in to the same spot of the defensive player he is replacing.

     Rule 7: Section: 2-d-2)-b), Page 63 – 64.
  2. If only one substitution is made, the new pitcher entering the game must bat in previous DH spot.

     Rule 7: Section: 2-d-2)-b)-(1), Page 63 – 64.
  3. If more than one substation is made, the coach must specify their positions in the batting order.

     Rule 7: Section: 2-d-2)-b)-(2), Page 63 – 64.

- A defensive player becomes the pitcher, and the DH is terminated.

  Rule 7: Section: 2-d-7)-a), Page 64.

  Results: The defensive player's old position can then be filled by the terminated DH.

  Rule 7: Section: 2-d-7)-b), Page 64.

Ten-Player Lineup, Pinch Hitter or Runner

- The DH can be pinch hit or run for at any time. That pinch hitter or runner then becomes the new DH.
    1. The new DH can enter as pitcher during this substitution.

       Rule 7: Section: 2-d-3)-a), Page 64.
    2. When the DH does enter as pitcher, the replaced pitcher cannot return in any capacity.

       Rule 7: Section: 2-d-3)-a)-(2), Page 64.
- A pitcher can pinch hit or pinch run only for the DH, he is considered the new DH and the DH is not terminated.
    1. The pitcher may then later be replaced as the DH and remain as pitcher.

       Rule 7: Section: 2-d-4)-a), Page 64.
- Once a pinch hitter bats for any player in the batting order and enters into the game to pitch, the DH's role is terminated for the remainder of the game.

  Rule 7: Section: 2-d-1-e), Page 63.

DH & P/DH Author's Overview

The NCAA, DH and P/DH applicable rules are determined by what the coach decides to submit on his starting player lineup card. At pregame, the coach has two options and both of those options after the game starts could be switched or terminated.

Option One:

A coach can submit a starting nine-player lineup card with no DH listed. "It is not mandatory that a designated hitter bat for the pitcher," but when the pitcher is listed in the batting order, he automatically becomes the DH.

Rule 7: Section: 2-c, Page 63.

- As both the pitcher and DH, the player is considered the P/DH and can be substituted for as such.

  Rule 7: Section: 2-c, Page 63.

- The nine-player lineup P/DH can switch to a ten-player lineup, with the DH batting for the pitcher who is moved into the non-batting ten-spot as stated below:

  1. A ten-player lineup is created when the P/DH remains as pitcher, while being replaced with a new designated hitter.

     Rule 7: Section: 2-e-3)-a), Page 65.

  2. A ten-player lineup is created when the P/DH remains only as a designated hitter, while being replaced by a new pitcher.

     Rule 7: Section: 2-e-1)-a)-(1), Page 65.

  3. When the P/DH is ejected, the coach can switch to a ten-player lineup with a designated hitter and a non-batting pitcher listed in the tenth spot or continue as a P/DH in a nine-player lineup.

     Rule 7: Section: 2-e-4)-a), Page 65.

- A DH is terminated in a nine-player lineup when:
  1. A P/DH is moved to a defensive position.

     Rule 7: Section: 2-e-2), Page 65.
  2. A defensive player becomes the pitcher, replacing the P/DH.

     Rule 7: Section: 2-e-5, Page 65.
  3. A pinch hitter bats for any player and then enters the game to pitch the DH is terminated.

     Rule 7: Section: 2-d-1)-e), Page 63.

Option Two:

A coach can submit a starting ten-player lineup card with DH listed in the batting order and the pitcher listed in the non-batting ten-spot.

- The ten-player lineup can revert back to a nine-player lineup as follows.
  1. When the DH is ejected, the DH spot is not terminated and can be replaced with another player.

     Rule 7: Section: 2-d-9)-a), Page 65.
  2. The pitcher may become the P/DH at this time, then all nine-player lineup rules shall apply from this point forward.

     Rule 7: Section: 2-d-9-b), Page 65.

- A DH is terminated in a ten-player lineup when:
  1. A pinch hitter bats for any player and then enters the game to pitch, the DH is terminated.

     Rule 7: Section: 2-d-1)-e), Page 63.
  2. A DH enters the game as a defensive player, the DH is terminated.

     Rules 7: Section: 2-d-5-a), Page 64.
  3. A pitcher is moved to a defensive position, the DH is terminated.

     Rule 7: Section: 2-d-2)-a), Page 63 – 64.
  4. A defensive player becomes the pitcher, the DH is terminated.

     Rule 7: Section: 2-d-7)-a), Page 64.

Infield Fly Rule

As with every chapter in this book, infield fly rule in effect rulings have been collected, converted into Basic English and listed in sequence and order of importance. The twist with this topic is the multiple numbers of variables where the "umpire's judgement" comes into play, depending upon where the infield fly lands, bounces, is hit, caught, dropped, or whether it is near a foul line. You can have converging players or a fly ball carrying out into the infield. Nothing is clear cut on an infield fly, so we offer insight on what to look out for and take into consideration that other rule books do not offer.

Definition of an Infield Fly in Effect

- There must be less than two outs with baserunners on first and second or first, second, and third base.
- It must be a fair fly ball that can be (not is) caught with ordinary effort by either a pitcher, catcher, infielder, or outfielder positioned in the infield during the play.
- Line drives or an attempted bunt are not an infield fly.
- A called infield fly is a live ball and runners can advance at their own risk.
- When an infield fly ball is in effect and lands uncaught foul, the called infield fly is ignored.

Rule 2: Section: 48, Page 29.

Definition of a Fair Ball

- A legally batted ball is a fair ball when:
    1. It stops on fair territory between home plate and first or third bases.

       Rule 2: Section: 27-a, Page 27.
    2. Bounds past first or third base while on or over fair territory.

       Rule 2: Section: 27-b, Page 27.
    3. It touches any base or falls on fair territory on or beyond first or third base, including the foul poles.

       Rule 2: Section: 27-c, Page 27.
    4. While over fair territory, the ball touches a player, umpire, or any piece of equipment.

       Exception: A batted ball that hits the pitcher's plate and goes between first and home or third and home in foul territory is a foul ball.

       Rule 2: Section: 27-d, Page 27.

Infield Fly in Effect Rulings

- The batter is out when an infield fly in effect is declared by an umpire.

Rule 7: Section: 11-j, Page 69.

- With an infield fly in effect, when the ball hits a runner who is in contact with a base, that runner is not out.

Rule 8: Section: 5-k, Note 1, Page 79.

- With an infield fly in effect, when the ball hits a runner who is not in contact with a base, both the baserunner and batter-runner are out.

  Result: It is an immediate dead ball.

Rule 8: Section: 5-k, Note 1, Page 79.

- With an infield fly in effect, when the ball is intentionally dropped or allowed to fall untouched, the batter is out, and the ball is live and in play. Runners do not have to tag up and can run at their own risk.

Rule 7: Section: 11-q, Note, Page 70.

Author's Notes for Infield Fly in Effect

- Prior to calling infield fly, experienced umpires are taught to observe the defense in order to establish ordinary effort.
- It may also be helpful to observe the baserunners. Baserunners' actions can also help indicate when you do or do not have an infield fly. When baserunners are standing on or near their bases believing the ball is caught, it is usually a strong indication that you have an infield fly.
- In reality, any fly ball can be caught with ordinary effort particularly with skilled players as long as they are in a proximity near or under the ball. By applying this logic, even when the player is having trouble (wind) playing the ball or back peddling onto the grass, it is still theoretically possible to establish ordinary effort.
- With an infield fly scenario on a very windy day while runners are holding their bases believing the ball is caught, understand the following:
    1. When you call an infield fly, the batter-runner is out, and the defense might drop the ball.
    2. When you do not call an infield fly and the ball is not caught landing in fair ground, the play can result in a game- or inning-ending double or triple play.

Section Continued on Page 78

- An infield fly ball dropping near a foul line is problematic because it can be caught, dropped, bounce, or roll into either fair or foul territory. With an infield fly in effect landing near a foul line, you should do these things before making the next call:
  1. Point up at the ball.
  2. Verbally declare, "Infield Fly when Fair."
  3. Wait to see where, when, or if it's touched, also where it lands and stops.
- When an infield fly is in effect and dropping near a foul line, the following things can happen which results in batter-runner being out:
  1. The ball is caught in fair territory.
  2. The ball is touched or dropped while in fair territory.
  3. The ball lands untouched and hits a base before going foul.
  4. The ball lands untouched in fair ground on or beyond a base before rolling foul.
  5. The ball lands foul in front of a base before bouncing untouched back into fair territory where it is either touched or stops in fair territory.

Batter's Interference

Batter's interference has to be a good candidate for the least understood infractions in baseball. It seems that every time this infraction takes place and rulings are enforced, many players, coaches, or fans lose their minds. We have collected, organized, and listed rulings in sequence and order of importance together so that you see every step needed to apply correct rulings. This is another play that, when you apply all the correct rulings, coaches will show you more respect, and the your game will be smoother.

Rulings

- Batter's interference is when the batter intentionally or unintentionally interferes with the catcher's fielding or throwing by:
    1. Stepping out of the batter's box.
    2. Making any other movement that hinders a defensive player's (catcher's) actions at home plate.

    Rule 7: Section: 11-f, Page 68.

    Result: The batter is out and runners return to bases at the time of the pitch.

    Rule 7: Section: 11-f, Penalty, Page 68.

- Batter's interference with an attempt to put out a runner at a base is successful.

    Results:

    1. The batter's interference is ignored and the batter is not out, unless he strikes out during the infraction.
    2. The ball stays live and runners may advance.

    Rule 6: Section: 3-b, Penalty-3, Page 59.

- The attempt to put out a runner is unsuccessful because of batter's interference.

    Results:

    1. It is an immediate dead ball.
    2. The batter is out.
    3. All runners return to the bases occupied at the time of pitch.

    Rule 6: Section: 3-b- Penalty 3, Page 59.

- When there is batter's interference with less than two outs and a play on a runner at home plate, that runner is called out, not the batter.

  Rule 7: Section: 11-f, Exception 1), Page 68.

  Results:

  1. When there is batter's interference and any runner attempting to advance is put our, the batter is not out.
  2. When there is batter's interference and the runner that is trying to score has been called out, the batter is not out.

  Rule 7: Section: 11-f, Exception 2), Page 68.

- When there is batter interference with a play at the plate and less than two out, then the runner is out.

  Rule 8: Section: 5-l, Page 79.

- When there is batter interference with a play at the plate and two out, then the batter is out and the run does not score.

  Rule 8: Section: 5-l, Page 79.

Catcher's Return Throw to Pitcher Rulings

- If the batter unintentionally interferes with the catcher's return throw to the pitcher that hits the batter or his bat while the batter is in the batter's box and no runners are stealing, the following happens:

  Rule 7: Section: 11-f, Exception 4, Note, Page 68 – 69.

  1. The batter is not out.

     Rule 7: Section: 11-f, Exception 4, Note, Page 68 – 69.

  2. The ball stays live and in play.

     Rule 7: Section: 11-f, Exception, Note, Page 68 – 69.

- When the batter unintentionally interferes with the catcher's return throw to the pitcher which then hits the batter or his bat while the batter is legally out of the batter's box and no runners are stealing.

  Results:

  1. The batter is not out.
  2. It is an immediate dead ball and runners return.

  Rule 7: Section: 11-f, Exception 4, Note, Page 68 – 69.

Backswing and Follow-through Rulings

Author's Note: any actions of the bat after the initial attempt to hit a pitch, being referred to as either follow-through or backswing have the same meaning in the NCAA rule book.

- After swinging at a pitch, missing and, continuing his backswing, hits the catcher or the ball, the following happens:
    1. The pitch is a strike.
    2. The ball becomes dead.
    3. No runners will advance.

Rule 6: Section: 2-d, Page 58.

- A batter's follow-through, on the third strike, hits the catcher and causes the catcher to drop the ball.
    1. The ball is dead.
    2. The batter is out on third strike, not interference.
    3. No runners can advance.

Rule 6: Section: 2-d-1, Page 58.

- While in the box, when the batter's normal follow-through unintentionally strikes the catcher attempting to throw out a runner the following happens:
    1. When the runner is put out, the play stands.
    2. When the runner is not put out, time is called.
    3. Runners must return.

Rule 6: Section: 2-d-2), Page 58.

Interference

Interference is one word that entails the possibility of any one of dozens of infractions caused by just about anyone in or around a baseball game. Umpires, coaches, spectators, base runners, and batters are all subject to interfering with live play intentionally or unintentionally, with a pitched ball, a batted ball, or thrown ball, verbally or physically, and it is up to the umpire to be aware of these dozens of infractions and apply the appropriate rulings. In this chapter, we have once again converted rule book language into basic English, collected, and put related infractions and rulings together so that it is not only easier to find, but easier to study, retain, and apply.

Definition of Interference

- An offensive player, umpire, or non-game person interferes in the following ways:
  1. Verbally or physically hinders (no contact needed) any fielder attempting to make a play.
  2. Confuses or impedes any fielder attempting to make a play.

Rule 2: Section: 51, Page 29.

> Author's Note: The word "hinder" by definition means "to create difficulties for someone, resulting in delay or blocking". Other synonyms: hamper, frustrate, or set back.

Defensive-Catcher's Interference

- When any defensive player, usually the catcher interferes with the batter's swing or prevents the batter from striking at a pitch.

  Rule 8: Section: 2-e, Page 72.

  1. When a play follows the interference, the offensive team may ignore the interference and accept the outcome of the play.
  2. When the batter reaches first base and all other runners advance at least one base, the interference is ignored.

  Rule 8: Section: 2-e-1, Page 72.

- When a play continues immediately after the interference, the offensive team can select to either accept the interference or the outcome of the play. The interference is ignored when all other runners advance one base and the batter reaches first base.

  Rule 8: Section: 2-e-1, Page 72.

- Any runners attempting to steal during catcher interference with the batter's swing will be awarded the base the player was attempting to steal.

  1. When the base runner is not attempting to steal during catcher interference, that runner is not awarded the base unless he is forced by the batter's interference.

  Rule 8: Section: 2-e-2, Page 72.

Defensive-Catcher's Interference Squeeze Play Rulings

- On an attempted squeeze play or steal of home plate, it is catcher's interference when the catcher—without the ball—steps on or in front of home plate or touches the batter or bat. It is a balk on the pitcher.

  Rule 8: Section: 3-p, Page 75.

  Results:

  1. It is an immediate dead ball.
     a. The batter is awarded first base on the interference.
  2. The run scores.
  3. It is a balk. All baserunners advance one base.

  Rule 8: Section: 3-p, Penalty, Page 75.

- When the batter's swing while loosening up preparing for a pitch hits the catcher or his glove, it is not catcher's interference and the following happens:
  1. Immediately call time.
  2. Neither a pitch nor swing is allowed.

  Rule 8: Section: 2-e, Note, Page 72.

Coach's Interference Rulings

- When a base coach assists a runner to or from a base.
  1. It is a delayed dead ball.
  2. After the play ends, the runner is called out.

     Rule 3: Section: 3-e, Penalty, Page 37.
  3. All other runners advance at their own risk.

     Rule 3: Section: 3-e, Note, Page 37.
- When a coach intentionally interferes with a thrown ball:
  1. It is an immediate dead ball.

     Rule 6: Section: 2-c, Page 58.
  2. The runner is out.

     Rule 8: Section: 3-j, Page 74.
  3. All runners return to the base last touched.

     Rule 6: Section: 2-c, Page 58.
     Rule 8: Section: 3-j, Page 74.
- When a coach is unintentionally hit by a thrown ball while in a foul ball area, the ball stays a live ball.

  Rule 8: Section: 3-j, Page 74.

Umpire's Interference Rulings

- When a fair-batted ball touches an umpire before it touches a fielder or passes all infielders (excluding the pitcher), the following happens:

  Rule 6: Section: 2-f, Page 58.

  1. It is an immediate dead ball.
  2. The batter-runner is awarded first base.
  3. No runners can advance, unless forced.

  Rule 6: Section: 2-f, Penalty Page 58.

- When a fair-batted ball hits a base umpire after it passes a fielder (excluding the pitcher), the ball remains live and in play.

  Rule 6: Section: 2-f, Penalty, Note, Page 58.

- When a fair-batted ball touches an umpire after it touches an infielder (including the pitcher), the ball remains live and in play.

  Rule 6: Section: 2-f, Penalty, Note, Page 58.

- When the plate umpire interferes with the catcher's attempt to throw, the following happens:

  Rule 6: Section: 3-a, Page 59.

  1. When a runner is called out on the catcher's throw, the interference is ignored.

     Rule 6: Section: 3-a, Note, Page 59.

  2. When a runner is not called out, runners return to the bases occupied at the time of the infraction.

     Rule 6: Section: 3-a, Page 59.

- When a pitched or thrown ball strikes an umpire, the ball remains live.

  Rule 6: Section: 1-b, Page 57.

  1. Base runners can advance at their own risk.

     Rule 8: Section: 3-i, Page 74.

Base Awards for Interference Rulings

Time-of-Pitch Base Awards

- When the batter-runner has not reached first base at the time of the interference, all runners return to the bases occupied at the time of the pitch.

Rule 2: Section: 51, Note 2, Page 29.

Time-of-Interference Base Awards

- When a batter, batter-runner, or baserunner is called out for interference, all other runners return to the bases last touched at the time of interference.

Rule 2: Section: 51, Note 1, Page 29.

- When there is an overruling play made on another runner, all runners return to the bases last touched at the time of interference.

Rule 2: Section: 51, Note 2, Page 29.

Interference-Runner or Running Lane

As soon as a batter puts a fair batted ball into live play, he becomes a batter-runner until he safely reaches first base. During this period between leaving the batter's box and reaching first base, there is a three-foot running lane the batter-runner has the choice to use or not use, at his own potential peril. Throws, batted balls, and the fielding of each can come into play the last forty-five feet of the first base line. Once the batter-runner rounds first base, he is then considered a runner and is again at risk of runner's interference for all the same reasons, excluding running lane rulings. We discuss what happens when a defensive player misplays an initial attempt at a batted ball. Does the runner interfere or is it obstruction? We explain the differences in basic English, so you can confidently and correctly make the calls when you see them.

Runner's Interference Rulings

- A runner is out for interference when:
  1. They intentionally interfere with a fielder attempting to field a batted ball.

     Rule 8: Section: 5-d, Page 78.
  2. They intentionally interfere with a throw or a thrown ball.

     Rule 8: Section: 5-d, Page 78.

     Result: It is an immediate dead ball. All other runners return to the last bases legally touched at the time of the interference.

     Rule 2: Section: 51, Note 1, Page 29.
- When a double play was likely and the runner intentionally interferes with a throw or fielding, the following happens:
  1. Both the runner and batter-runner are called out.

     Rule 8: Section: 5-d, Page 78.
  2. All other runners return to the last base legally touched at the time of the interference.

     Rule 2: Section: 51, Note 1, Page 29.
- When any runner intentionally interferes with a batted or thrown ball with a helmet or other equipment.

  Results:
  1. It is an immediate dead ball.
  2. The runner is out.
  3. Any runner in front of the interference returns to the base occupied at the time of interference.
  4. The batter-runner is awarded first base.

  Rule 6: Section: 2-h, Page 59.

- When the batter-runner has not touched first base at the time of interference, all runners shall return to the base last occupied at the time of the pitch.

  Rule 2: Section: 51, Note 2, Page 29.

- When a fielder misplays a batted ball and, while in the immediate reach of the misplayed ball, that fielder is then contacted by a baserunner, the baserunner is called out for interference.

  Rule 2: Section: 51, Note 3, Page 29.

- When the pitcher deflects a batted ball that can still be played by another fielder, that fielder is protected, and contact by a runner is still considered interference.

  Rule 8: Section: 5-d, Note 2, Page 78.

Misplayed Ball—Interference or Obstruction

- When a fielder is chasing after a misplayed batted ball (not in the immediate reach of the misplayed ball and he contacts the runner it is obstruction.

Rule 2: Section: 51, Note 4, Page 31.
Rule 2: Section: 55, Note 2, Page 30.

Three-Foot Running Lane Rulings

- Running lane interference is when, beginning half way to first base, the batter-runner steps outside of the run lane in either fair or foul ground with either foot and interferes by:

Rule 7: Section: 11-p, Page 69.
Rule 7: Section: 11-p, Note 2, Page 69.

1. Altering the throw of a fielder.
2. Hindering or altering a fielder's opportunity to field a throw.
3. Being hit by a throw that is made in an attempt to make a play.

Rule 7: Section: 11-p, Note 1, Page 69.

Results:

a. It is an immediate dead ball.

Rule 2: Section: 51, Notc 1, Page 29.

b. The batter-runner is out.

Rule 7: Section: 11-p, Note 1, Page 69.

c. All other runners return to the last base legally touched at the time of the interference.

Rule 2: Section: 51, Note 1, Page 29.

Ruling Continued on Page 98

Exceptions:

a. When the batter-runner is very near first base, he can exit the three-foot run lane by stepping, striding, reaching, or sliding in an attempt to:

    I. Touch first base.

    II. Avoid a tag.

Rule 7: Section: 11-p, Exception, Page 69.

b. The batter-runner can run outside the run lane at any time to avoid contact with a player fielding a ball.

Rule 7: Section: 11-p, Page 69.

c. The batter-runner may step out of running lane in the immediate proximity of first base as long as he was in the lane prior to that point.

Rule 7: Section: 11-p, Exception, Page 69.

Runner Hit by a Fair Batted Ball is Out When:

- A fair batted ball hits the runner, including a runner in contact with a base, before it has touched a fielder, including the pitcher.

  Rule 8: Section: 5-k, Page 79.

  Results:

  1. It is an immediate dead ball.

     Rule 6: Section: 2-e-Penalty, Page 58.
  2. The runner who was hit is out.

     Rule 8: Section: 2-g, Page 72.
     Rule 6: Section: 2-e, Page 58.
  3. The batter-runner is awarded first base.

     Rule 8: Section: 2-g, Page 72.
  4. No other runners may advance or score.

     Rule 6: Section: 2-e-Penalty, Page 58.

- A fair batted ball hits the runner, including a runner in contact with a base, before it has passed all infielders, excluding the pitcher, with a chance of making a play.

  Rule 8: Section: 5-k, Page 79.

  Results:

  1. It is an immediate dead ball.

     Rule 6: Section: 2-e-Penalty, Page 58.
  2. The runner who was hit is out.

     Rule 8: Section: 2-g, Page 72.
     Rule 6: Section: 2-e, Page 58.
  3. The batter-runner is awarded first base.

     Rule 8: Section: 2-g, Page 72.
  4. No other runners may advance or score.

     Rule 6: Section: 2-e-Penalty, Page 58.

- A fair batted ball goes through or by a defensive player, then strikes the runner, and a second defensive player was behind that runner. The umpire's believes the second defensive player could have made the play.

  Result: The runner is out for interference.

- An infield fly is in effect and the fly ball hits a runner that is not in contact with a base.

  Results:

  1. Both the base runner who was hit and the batter-runner are out and
  2. The ball is dead.

Rule 8, Section: 5-k-Note 1, Page 79.

Runner Hit by a Fair Batted Ball is Not Out When:

- A fair batted ball goes through or by an infielder, or the ball is deflected by any fielder, then hits the runner.

  Rule 6: Section: 2-e, Note, Page 58.

  Exception: The ball has passed one defensive player, then strikes the runner, and a second defensive player was behind that runner. When the umpire believes the player could have made a play, the runner is out.

  Rule 6: Section: 2-e, Note, Page 58.

- An infield fly is in effect and the fly ball hits a runner who is touching a base. The runner is not out.

  Rule 8: Section: 5-k, Note 1, Page 79.

Obstruction

Obstruction in baseball is many things. It can be extremely obvious, as when a runner is physically knocked to the ground while running the bases, or it can be as subtle as an infielder brushing the arm of a base runner. In all cases, knowing what to do is extremely important. When infractions take place, everyone is excited, noise elevates, and confusion can overcome many. Obstruction is no exception. Excited teams and fans immediately either want the umpire to intervene or play to continue and the umpire is supposed to appease everyone. This chapter provides a format that, when studied, can be retained and, while not appeasing all, correct rulings can be applied.

Definition of Obstruction

- Obstruction by definition is when a defensive player without the ball or who is "in the act of fielding a ball" impedes the progress of any runner. There are two different types of Obstruction, Type 1 Obstruction and Type 2 Obstruction.
    1. Type 1 Obstruction is committed against a runner on which a play is being made.
    2. Type 2 Obstruction is committed against a runner on which no play is being made.

Rule 2: Section: 55, Page 30.

Exception: When a batter-runner is obstructed after putting a batted ball into play, it can either Type 1 or Type 2 Obstruction.

Rule 6: Section: 3-d, Page 59.
Rule 6: Section: 3-d-1), Page 59.
Rule 6: Section: 3-d-2), Page 59.
Rule 6: Section: 3-d-3), Page 59.

Type 1 Obstruction Rulings

- A Type 1 Obstruction is when the runner is obstructed as the defense is making a play on him.

  Rule 2: Section: 55, Page 30.

  Example: While in a run down, the runner is knocked to the ground by the short stop as the third baseman is attempting to apply a tag with the ball. This is a Type 1 Obstruction and the following would happen:

  1. The umpire would point and call, "That's obstruction."
  2. It is an immediate dead ball; the umpire then calls time.
  3. The obstructed runner receives at least one base past the last legally touched base before the obstruction.
  4. All other runners are awarded the bases they would have reached without the obstruction.

  Rule 2: Section: 55, Page 30.

  Authors Note: A runner caught in a rundown is frequently subject to Type 1 Obstruction simply because of the multiple numbers of defensive players involved in or near the base path. Umpires can become so intent on looking for a tag that the obstruction can be easily missed.

- The defensive player may not block any part of a base with any part of his body unless he has clear possession of the ball, the following happens:

  1. It is an immediate dead ball.
  2. The umpire calls time.
  3. The obstructed runner receives at least one base past the last legally touched base before the obstruction.

  Rule 8: Section: 3-e-1), Note, Page 73.

- The catcher, without the ball, has no right to block the path of the runner trying to score.

  Rule 2: Section: 55, Note 6, Page 31.

- When a runner is attempting to score, the catcher can only be in his path when:
  1. The catcher is fielding the ball.
  2. When a fielder (catcher) is in position to receive a thrown ball, he may be considered legal and "in the act of fielding" a ball, even while in the path of a runner. It is entirely the umpire's judgement.
  3. The catcher has the ball in his hand.

  Rule 2: Section: 55, Note 6, Page 31.

Type 2 Obstruction Rulings

- A Type 2 Obstruction is when the runner is obstructed while no play is being made on him.

  Rule 2: Section: 55, Page 30.

  Example: The batter-runner hits a ball is deep in the left center gap and the batter-runner rounding first base is tripped by the first baseman. This is a Type 2 Obstruction.

- The following happens when a Type 2 Obstruction occurs:
  1. The umpire points and calls, "That's obstruction."
  2. It is a delayed dead ball. Let play continue.
  3. When play stops or the obstructed runner is tagged out, time is called and bases are awarded that would nullify the obstruction.

  Rule 8: Section: 3-e-2), Note, Page 73.
  Rule 2: Section: 55, Page 30.

Batter-Runner Obstructed

- There are three types of plays that impact rulings for a batter-runner being obstructed before reaching first base.
  Rule 6: Section: 3-d, Page 59.

1. A ground ball is hit to infielder, and the batter-runner is obstructed running to first.

   Results:

   a. Immediate dead ball.

   b. Batter-runner is awarded first base.

   Rule 6: Section: 3-d-1), Penalty, Page 59.

2. A line drive or pop-up is hit and the batter-runner is obstructed running to first.

   Results:

   a. The umpire calls, "That's obstruction."

   b. It is a delayed dead ball, and the ball stays live.

   c. When the ball is caught, the batter is out.

   d. When the ball is dropped, the umpire calls time and bases are awarded that would nullify the obstruction.

   Rule 6: Section: 3-d-2), Penalty, Page 59.

3. A ball is hit to the outfield and the batter-runner is obstructed running to first.

   Results:

   a. The umpire points and calls, "That's obstruction."
   b. It is a delayed dead ball; the ball stays live until all play ceases, then the umpire calls time.
   c. When the ball is caught, the batter is out and the obstruction is ignored.
   d. When the ball is dropped, wait until play stops. The umpire calls time and bases are awarded.
   e. When runner advances past base award and is put out, the out stands.

Rule 6: Section: 3-d-3), Penalty, Page 59.

Misplayed Ball—Obstruction or Interference

- When a fielder receiving a thrown ball and the ball directly toward and near enough to the fielder that he must occupy his position in order to catch the throw, he is considered in the act of field the ball.

  Rule 2: Section: 55, Note 1, Page 30.

- When a fielder misses a fielded or thrown ball and is then in pursuit of the ball, he is no longer considered "in the act of fielding the ball."

  Rule 2: Section: 55, Note 2, Page 30.

- After a fielder has misplayed a batted ball and the ball is within a step and a reach the fielder is still considered "in the act of fielding the ball."

  Rule 2: Section: 55, Note 3, Page 30.

  1. A runner contacting a fielder within a step and a reach of a batted ball will be called out for.

     Rule 2: Section: 51, Note 3, Page 30.

- During a play at any base, the defensive player must have clear possession of the ball before he can block the base, otherwise it is obstruction.

  Rule 2: Section: 55-Note 4, Page 30..

- When a fielder attempts to catch a wild throw and the ball is misplayed by the fielder who then tangles with the runner, the fielder cannot further hinder the runner.

  Rule 2: Section: 51, Note 5, 31.

Pitching Positions and Substitutions

With only two positions for the pitcher to begin pitching from, this should be a simple and easy topic to cover. Quite the opposite is true, because after the pitcher establishes which of the two positions he will pitch from, just about every element of the pitcher's body is restricted or required to do or not do specific actions. The pitcher's defensive actions are regulated more heavily than any other defensive player.

Set Position Rulings

- A pitcher shows he is going to pitch from the set position when he does the following:
  1. The pitcher's chest faces a foul line.
  2. His pivot foot is in front of or on the pitcher's plate while touching the pitcher's plate.
     a. His pivot food must also be parallel to the pitcher's plate.
  3. His free foot is ahead of the pitcher's plate.
  4. The ball is in the pitcher's hand or glove at his side or on his hip before coming set.

  Rule 9: Section: 1-b, Page 84.

- When the pitcher comes set, he holds the ball in both hands in front of his body and comes to a complete, discernible, and obvious stop.

  Rule 9: Section: 1-b, Page 84.

- With runners on base and prior to any pitching motion, he can throw to a base without disengaging the pitching plate.

  Rule 9: Section: 1-a-4), Page 83.

  1. Violation of this rule with runners on is a balk.
  2. Violation of this rule with no runners is a no-pitch.

  Rule 9: Section: 1-a-4), Penalty, Page 84.

- The pitcher must be in contact with the pitcher's plate while taking his signs.

  Rule 9: Section: 2-j, Page 87.

  1. When the pitcher violates this rule, a ball is awarded the batter.
  2. When this violation happens and a pitch is thrown and the batter reaches first base or runners reach at least one base before possibly being put out, the violation is ignored.

  Rule 9: Section: 2-j, Penalty, Page 87.

- After taking his signs, the pitcher can use any ordinary motion, such as the stretch, before coming set.

  Rule 9: Section: 1-b, Page 84.

- The pitcher must use a continuous hand motion and cannot stop and start while coming to the set position.

  Rule 9: Section: 1-b, Page 84.

- When no one is on base, the pitcher does not need to come to a complete and discernible stop.

  Rule 9: Section: 1-b-2), Note 2, Page 84.

- The pitcher must step directly and gain ground toward the base in an attempt to pick off a runner.

  Rule 9: Section: 1-a-6), Page 83 – 84.

  1. Violation of this rule with runners on, is a balk

     Rule 9: Section: 1-a-6), Penalty, Page 84.

  2. Definition of directly as applied to this rule: a 45-degree angle gauging from the pivot foot to the base where the throw or feint is directed.

     Rule 9: Section: 1-a-6), Page 83 – 84.

- In either the windup or set position, the pitcher's pivot foot must be in contact with the pitcher's plate while taking signs from the catcher. A ball shall be awarded each time a pitcher violates this rule.

  Rule 9: Section: 1-f, Page 85.

- The pitcher must pitch from whichever position—set or windup—he took the catcher's signs. A ball shall be awarded each time a pitcher violates this rule.

  Rule 9: Section: 1-f, Page 85.

Windup Position Rulings

- A pitcher is in the windup position when he does the following:
    1. The pitcher stands chest and shoulders facing the batter.
    2. The pitcher's pivot foot can be in front of or on the pitcher's plate, but the foot must be in contact with the pitcher's plate.
    3. The non-pivot foot is touching or behind the front edge line extended outward from the pitching plate.

    Rule 9: Section: 1-a, Page 83.

    Penalty:

    a. First violation is a warning.

    b. Second violation is an illegal pitch. When no runners are on base, the umpire awards a ball. With runners on base, it's a balk.

    Rule 9: Section: 1-a, Penalty, Page 83.

- When the pitcher starts to deliver his pitch from the windup, he cannot stop or alter his delivery. He must pitch to the batter.

    Rule 9: Section: 1-a, Page 83.

    Penalty:

    1. First violation is a warning.
    2. Second violation is an illegal pitch. The umpire awards a ball.

    Rule 9: Section: 1-a, Penalty, Page 83.

- The pitcher cannot raise his feet from the ground, except in his delivery of the ball to the batter.

  Rule 9: Section: 1-a, Page 83.

  Penalty:

  1. First violation is a warning.
  2. Second violation is an illegal pitch, awarded a ball.

  Rule 9: Section: 1-a, Penalty, Page 83.

- The pitcher's free foot can take one step backward, sideward, or forward.

  Rule 9: Section: 1-a, Page 83.

- From the windup position a pitcher's hands can be:

  1. Together in front of the body, then begin his delivery.

     Rule 9: Section: 1-a-1-a), Page 83.

  2. Apart with throwing arm at side or both arms at his sides, then begin his delivery.

     Rule 9: Section: 1-a-1-b), Page 83.

  3. Apart and brings hands together, stopping before beginning his delivery.

     Rule 9: Section: 1-a-1-c), Page 83.

     Penalty:

     a. Violation for one of these three rules with runners on is a balk.

     b. Violation for one of these rules with no runners on is a no pitch.

     Rule 9: Section: 1-a-4), Penalty-1 – 7, Page 84.

- With runners on base, once a pitcher begins his delivery, the pitcher must pitch to the batter.

  Rule 9: Section: 1-a-2), Page 83.

  Penalty:

  1. Violation of this rule with runners on is a balk.
  2. Violation of this rule with no runners is a no pitch.

  Rule 9: Section: 1-a-4), Penalty 1 – 7, Page 84.

- From the windup with runners on base prior to any motion associated with the pitcher's delivery, the pitcher can disengage from the pitcher's plate.

  Rule 9: Section: 1-a-3), Page 83.

  Penalty:

  1. Violation of this rule with runners on is a balk.
  2. Violation of this rule with no runners is a no pitch.

  Rule 9: Section: 1-a-4), Penalty 1 – 7, Page 84.

- With runners on base, prior to any motion associated with the pitcher's delivery, he can throw to a base without disengaging the pitching plate.

  Rule 9: Section: 1-a-4), Page 83.

  Penalty:

  1. Violation of this rule with runners on is a balk.
  2. Violation of this rule with no runners is a no pitch.

  Rule 9: Section: 1-a-4), Penalty 1 – 7, Page 84.

- In order for the pitcher to change from windup to set position, he must first legally disengage.

Rule 9: Section: 1-a-5), Page 83.

Penalty:

1. Violation of this rule with runners on is a balk.
2. Violation of this rule with no runners is a no pitch.

Rule 9: Section: 1-a-5, Penalty 1 – 7, Page 84.

Pitcher Substitution

- Before substituting (replacing) a pitcher, one of the following must happen:
  1. The pitcher must retire the first opposing batter or that batter's substitute.
  2. The first opposing batter or that batter's substitute advances to first base or is put out.
  3. The side is retired.
  4. The pitcher is injured or ill; he may be replaced immediately.

  Rule 5: Section: 5-b, Page 46.
- A pitcher who is removed but remains in the game can return to pitch only once.

  Rule 5: Section: 5-b, Note 1, Page 46.

Slide

A legal slide in Major League Baseball conjures up visions of the baserunner going out of his way to make a hard slide into a fielder in order to break up a double play. We have all watched many times in amazement as second basemen and shortstops come up limping and rubbing bleeding shins and knees due to contact during a slide. Not in the NCAA. Slide rules in this book are focused on baserunners avoiding contact by clearly illustrating where a runner can slide, what he can or cannot do during a slide, and the penalties for failing to comply with a ruling.

Legal Slide Rulings

- Head first slide.

  Rule 8: Section: 4-a-1), Page 76.

- Feet first slide, one leg and buttock on ground before the base.

  Rule 8: Section: 4-a-1), Page76.

- Contact with a fielder is legal when the fielder makes a legal slide directly into the base and extended baseline or, during a pop-up slide, contact can occur on top of the base.

  Rule 8: Section: 4-b, Page 76.

- Any force-play slide must be on the ground before the base and in a direct line between two bases.

  Rule 8: Section: 4-a, Page 75.

  Exception: The runner can slide or run away from making contact with or altering the play of the defensive player.

  Rule 8: Section: 4-a, Exception, Page 76.

- All body parts, feet, legs, trunk, and arms must stay in a direct line between the two bases in order to be considered legally sliding "directly into a base".

  Rule 8: Section: 4-a-1), Page 76.

  Author's Note: The two official rule book phrases "in a direct line between the two bases" and "directly into a base" have the same meaning.

- It is a legal slide when the runner's momentum carries him through, over, and beyond while maintaining contact with the base in the baseline extended.

  Rule 8: Section: 4-a, Page 75.

Slide Ruling Illustration

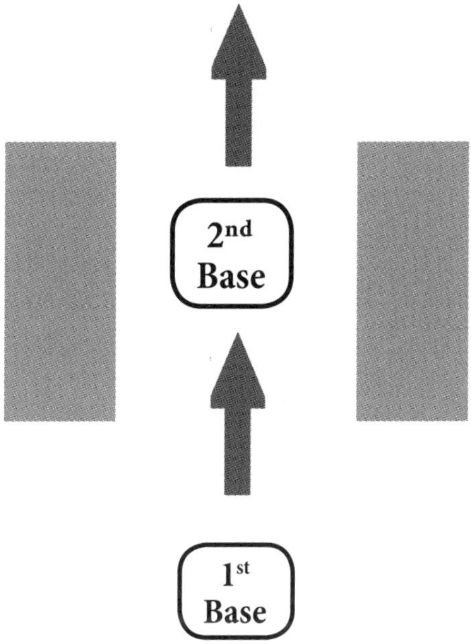

- While a runner is making a legal slide directly into a base and contact is made as the result of a pop-up slide, interference will not be called.

Rule 8: Section: 4-b, Page 76.

- It is a legal slide when the runner's entire body slides in a direct straight line between bases and his momentum can carry him through over and beyond while maintaining contact with the base in the baseline extended.

Rule 8: Section: 4-a, Page 75.
Rule 8: Section: 4-b, Page 76.

Author's Note: Gray boxes denote defense's area of protection. It is runner's interference when the runner's feet, legs, arms or trunk makes contact or not and alters the play of the fielder in the dark gray areas.

Rule 8: Section: 4-c-1), Page 76.

Illegal Slide Rulings

- Illegal sliding actions by a runner is called when:
    1. The runner slides or runs out of the base line towards the fielder with or without contact and alters fielder's play.

       Rule 8: Section: 4-c-1), Page 76.

    2. The runner uses a rolling or cross body slide and makes contact with or alter the play of the fielder.

       Rule 8: Section: 4-c-2), Page 77.

    3. The runner's raised leg makes contact higher than the fielder's knee when the fielder were in a standing position.

       Rule 8: Section: 4-c-3), Page 77.

    4. The runner slashes or kicks the fielder.

       Rule 8: Section: 4-c-4), Page 77.

    5. A runner makes an illegal slide or makes illegal contact with a fielder, even when there is no attempt by the fielder to throw in order to complete a play.

       Rule 8: Section: 4-c-5), 79.
       Rule 2: Section: 51, Note 1, 31.

       Penalties for illegal slides one through five are:

        a. With less than two outs, the batter-runner and the interfering runner are both out. No runners advance.

        b. With two outs, the interfering runner is out and no other runners may advance.

       Rule 8: Section: 4-c-1) – 5), Penalty, Page 77.

    6. The runner's slide or collision is flagrant, resulting in the runner being ejected.

       Rule 8: Section: 4-c-1) – 5), Penalty-3, Page 77.

Force-Play-Slide Rule

- During a force-play with a two-man umpiring crew and no play at home plate, the plate umpire should move towards the base where the force play is happening. It is primarily the home plate umpire's interference call.

  Note: The base umpire's primary responsibility is to follow the throw. This diminishes his ability to see the runner's interference.

  Rule 8: Section: 4-c, Note 2, Page 77.

- On a force-play-slide rule the lead runner has three legal options:

  1. The runner can make a legal slide by sliding on the ground before the base and in a direct line between the two bases.

     a. It is a legal slide when his momentum carries him through, over, and beyond while maintaining contact with the base in the baseline extended.

     Rule 8: Section: 4-a, Page 75.

     b. While making a legal slide into a base, contact with a fielder and contact at eh end of a pop-up slide are both legal.

     Rule 8: Section: 4-b, Page 76.

  3. The runner can slide away from the defensive player in order to avoid making contact or altering the play.

     Rule 8: Section: 4-a, Exception, Page 78.

  4. The runner can run away from the defensive player in order to avoid making contact or altering the play.

     Rule 8: Section: 4-a, Exception, Page 78.

- When a Force-Play-Slide Rule is in effect with less than two outs, the completion of a double play is not needed to call both the forced runner and the batter-runner out.

  Rule 8: Section: 4, Page 75.

- The Force-Play-Slide Rule is an interference rule that ensures player's safety.

  Rule 8: Section: 4, Page 75.

- A Force-Play-Slide Rule can be called at all bases, regardless of the number of outs.

  Rule 8: Section: 4, Page 75.

- When there are two outs while a Force-Play-Slide Rule is in effect, the interfering runner is out and no runner advances.

  Rule 8: Section: 4-c, Penalty 1 – 5, Page 77.

- When bases are loaded with no outs while a Force-Play-Slide Rule is in effect and interference is called, all other runners must return to their bases.

  Rule 8: Section: 4-c, Note 1, Page 77.

Collision Rule—Flagrant or Malicious Contact

- The intent of this rule is to encourage baserunners and defensive players to avoid violent collisions.

  Rule 8: Section: 7, Page 81.

- When the defensive player has clear possession of the ball and blocks either the base path or the base or plate, the runner may then legally slide and make contact with the fielder as long as the runner is making a legitimate attempt to reach the base or plate.

  Rule 8: Section: 7-a, Page 81.

- The runner must make an actual attempt to reach the base or plate.

  Rule 8: Section: 7-a-1), Page 81.

- When the runner initiates an avoidable collision or attempts to dislodge the ball, the following happens:
  1. The runner is out, even if the ball is dropped.
  2. It is an immediate dead ball.
  3. All runners return to the base last touched at the time of the collision.

  Rule 8: Section: 7-a-1), Penalty, Page 81.

Section Continued on Page 128

- Contact above the waist is ruled by the umpire as an attempt by the runner to dislodge the ball. The runner may not attempt to dislodge the ball from the fielder. The following happens:

  Rule 8: Section: 7-a-2), Page 81.

  1. When the contact is ruled flagrant or malicious before the runner touches the base or plate, the runner is out and ejected.
  2. It is an immediate dead ball.
  3. All runners return to the base last touched at the time of the collision.

  Rule 8: Section: 7-a-2), Penalty, Page 81.

- The runner must attempt to avoid a collision when he can reach the base without a collision.

  Rule 8: Section: 7-a-3, Page 81.

  1. When the contact is rule flagrant or malicious after the runner touches the base or plate, the runner is safe and ejected.

     Results:

     a. It is an immediate dead ball.
     b. All runners return to the bases last touched at the time of the collision.

  Rule 8: Section: 7-a-3), Penalty, Page 81.

- A runner attempting to score cannot deviate his direct path to the plate in order to initiate avoidable contact with a defensive player.

  Rule 8: Section: 7-b, Page 81 – 82

- When the runner is determined to have deviated from his path and is in violation of the collision rule when he:
    1. Fails to make an effort to touch the plate.
    2. Lowers his shoulder.
    3. Pushes through the defensive player with his hands, elbows, or arms.
    4. Initiates a collision that could have been avoided.

        Results:

        a. The ball is dead.

        b. All baserunners return to the bases last touched at the time of the collision.

Rule 8: Section: 7-2, Page 81 – 82.

- A catcher violates the collision rule when:
    1. The catcher blocks the plate without possession of the ball and hinders or impedes the progress of the runner attempting to score.
    2. The catcher is not making a legitimate attempt to field the throw and hinders or impedes the progress of the runner attempting to score.

Rules 8: Section: 7-b, Note, Page 82.

- The catcher in clear possession of the ball, can block the pathway of the runner trying to score.

Rule 8: Section: 7-b), Page 81 – 82.

- When the catcher is in the legitimate act of fielding or reacting to a direction or hop of an imminent ball or catch thrown by a pitcher or infielder, the catcher is not in violation of the collision rule.

Rule 8: Section: 7-b, Page 81 – 82.

- When the catcher without the ball is not in violation of the collision rule when the runner could have avoided the collision by sliding.

  Rule 8: Section: 7-b, Page 81 – 82.

- Catchers who make unnecessary and forcible contact with a runner attempting to slide may be subject to being ejected.

  Rule 8: Section: 7-b), Page 81 – 82.

Substitutions Definition

Knowing when a player can enter the game legally is never as easy as it may seem. Is the player eligible or has he already been in the game? These are reasonable questions for which the umpire must provide the correct rulings. In this chapter, we have collected and converted these rulings into basic English so that when a player enters the game, you will know what to do and rule accordingly.

Substitution Rulings

- Before replacing a substitute for a pitcher, one of the following must happen:
    1. The pitcher retires the first opposing batter or that batter's substitute.
    2. The first opposing batter or that batter's substitute advances to first base or is put out.
    3. The side is retired.
    4. The pitcher is injured or ill; he may be replaced immediately.

  Rule 5: Section: 5-b, Page 46.

- When a pitcher is removed as a pitcher but stays in the game, he can return to pitch only once.

  Rule 5: Section: 5-b, Note 1, Page 46.

- A substitute becomes a player when reported to the UIC and recorded in the line-up.

  Rule 5: Section: 5-b, Note 2, Page 46.

- When a pitcher is brought into a game and has not faced one batter or retired the side when the game is stopped by weather, that pitcher may or may not continue pitching when the game is resumed.

  Rule 5: Section: 5-b, Note 3, Page 46.

- A player removed from a game that has been suspended may not return to the lineup when the game is restarted.

  Rule 5: Section: 5-b, Note 4, Page 46.

- Excluding the pitcher, whenever the ball is dead, any player can be substituted for.

  Rule 5: Section: 5-c, Page 46.

- When the pitcher is pulled but remains as DH, that change must be announced at the same time the player is removed as pitcher.

  Rule 5: Section: 5-c, Note, Page 46.

- When the DH enters the game on defense, he must bat in his same spot. The new pitcher will bat in the vacated player's spot.

  Rule 5: Section: 5-d, Page 46.

- When two or more defensive substitutions enter the game, the coach will designate to the UIC their spot in the batting order.
  1. When the coach fails to do so, the UIC will place them in the order.

  Rule 5: Section: 5-e, Page 46.

- A baserunner cannot be replaced by another player whose name has appeared in the lineup.

  Rule 5: Section: 5-f, Page 47.

  1. When a player who has been in the game substitutes for a runner and an appeal is made, the following will happen:
     a. The illegal substitute is declared out.
     b. When a runner has scored and the appeal was made before the next pitch the illegal substitute is declared out and the run is cancelled. The illegal substitute is disqualified from the game and advancing runners are legal.
     c. When the illegal substitute was the third out, no following runs score.

  Rule 5: Section: 5-f, Penalty, Page 47.

- There is no penalty for an unreported eligible substitute entering the game.

  Rule 5: Section: 5-g, Note, Page 47.

- Should there be no announcement of the substitution, the substitute becomes a legal player when:
    1. An eligible substitute runner takes the place of another baserunner.

       Rule 5: Section: 5-g-1, Page 47.
    2. Pitcher contacts the pitcher's plate.

       Rule 5: Section: 5-g-2, Page 47.
    3. An eligible substitute assumes the position that was occupied by the fielder he replaced and play begins.

       Rule 5: Section: 5-g-3, Page 47.
    4. A batter steps in the batter's box.

       Rule 5: Section: 5-g-4, Page 47.
- A substitute player must bat in the same spot in the batting order as the player he replaced.

  Rule 5: Section: 5-c, Page 46.
- There is no re-entry rule in college. After a player is removed from the line-up, he cannot re-enter.

  Rule 5: Section: 5-j-3, Page 47.

Illegal Substitute Rulings

- A non-eligible, disqualified player who enters or re-enters the game is an illegal substitution.

  Examples:

  1. The starting shortstop who has been substituted for and removed from the line-up re-enters the game.
  2. The starting shortstop who was ejected from the game re-enters the game.

  Rule 2: Section: 22, Page 23.

- When an offensive team enters an illegal substitute into the game and he is discovered as either the batter or runner by the umpire or defense, the illegal substitute is immediately out and disqualified from the game.

  Rule 5: Section: 5-j-1, Page 47.

- When an offensive illegal substitute should score a run before being discovered:
  1. The defense must make a legal appeal before the next pitch to the next batter of either team.
  2. The appeal would then invalidate the actions of the illegal substitute.

  Rule 5: Section: 5-j-1, Page 47.

- When it is discovered by either the umpire or offense that the defensive team enters an illegal substitute into the game, the illegal substitute is replaced immediately.

  Rule 5: Section: 5-j-2, Page 47.

- When a play happens prior to the defense's illegal substitute being discovered and it is appealed before the next pitch to either team, the offense has the option to let the play stand or have the last batter come to bat again with his pitch count prior to his last pitch.

  Rule 5: Section: 5-j-2, Page 47.

Warning-Ejections and Bench and Field Conduct

You know that every game is not going to be problem-free. You know that not all coaches will be understanding or good sports when things go wrong. You know the players and fans are going to test the limits of what you, as an umpire, are willing to accept or ignore. Knowing all these potentially problematic scenarios can show up at any given moment during a baseball game, we have provided information in this chapter that can prepare you to intervene before a small problem becomes a huge problem. Resolving these issues before they balloon into disaster should be your priority; waiting and believing they will go away or resolve on their own is where the real problems start.

Game Misconduct Rulings

- No individual or team by their actions incite or attempt to incite at any time unsportsmanlike conduct.

  Rule 5: Section: 15-a, Page 53.

- No individual or team can incite unsportsmanlike conduct by:
  1. Word, sign, or actions or by inciting spectators regarding an umpire's decision.

     Rule 5: Section: 15-a-1, Page 53.
  2. Calling "Time" or saying any other word or phrase or committing any act while the ball is in play for the obvious purpose of making the pitcher balk. When a balk does happen, it is nullified.

     Rule 5: Section: 15-a-2, Page 53.
  3. Standing in the batter's line of vision with deliberate unsportsmanlike intent and distracting the batter.

     Rule 5, Section: 15-a-3, Page 53.

     Penalty: The offender is ejected from the game. He also receives an additional one-game suspension.

     Rule 5: Section: 15-a-1 – 3, Penalty, Page 53.
  4. Continually arguing or excessively expressing themselves with prolonged actions or offensive language after an ejection.

     Rule 5: Section: 15-a-4, Page 53.

     Penalty: The offenders, after an ejection, will be given an addition two-game suspension.

     Rule 5: Section: 15-a-4, Penalty, Page 53.

- No individual or team can incite unsportsmanlike conduct by participating in a National Anthem standoff between teams. The umpire must eject any offender for violating the Coaching and Players' Code of Ethics.

  Rule 5: Section: 15-a-5, Page 53.

  Penalty: The UIC will warn the head coach of the offending teams immediately that, after the National Anthem, if any player or team personnel do not go to their dugouts, both the head coach and the offending persons will be ejected.

  Rule 5: Section: 15-a-5, Penalty, Page 55.

- Coaches-Misconduct Rule defines any act of unsportsmanlike conduct or unprofessional behavior that discredits intercollegiate athletics or the game.

  Specifically, a coach cannot remove the team from the field or refuse to continue play due to a dispute with a game official.

  Rule 5: Section: 15-b, Page 53 – 54.

  Penalty: the coach is suspended from the next two games. The UIC is responsible for reporting this act to the institution's director of athletics, the conference commissioner (if applicable), and the NCAA staff liaison to the Baseball Rules Committee.

  Rule 5: Section: 15-b, Penalty, Page 54.

Official Warning Rulings

- Any umpire shall eject any player, coach, manager, or trainer for violation of the Coaches and Players' Code of Ethics.

Rule 3: Section: 6-d, Page 37.

1. On a first offense, the umpire may give an official warning to the offending player, coach, or team before ejecting.

Rule 3: Section: 6-d, Note 1, Page 37.

- When the umpire gives an official warning, he should state the following:

1. "This is your official warning."
2. "If you continue, you leave me no option but to eject you."
3. Slang warnings such as: "Knock it off", "Not another word," or "I've heard enough" are not considered an official warning.

Rule 2: Section: 57, Page 31.

Verbal Abuse (Bench Jockeying) Rulings

- Any member associated with a team using language that refers to or reflects negatively on opposing players, coaches, umpires, or spectators including coordinated actions used to distract, intimidate, or unnerve the opposing team or show poor sportsmanship by dugout personnel is subject to the following:

  Penalties:

  1. First offense: warning.
  2. Second offense: ejection.
  3. Third offense: the head coach ejected with offenders.

Rule 5: Section: 17, Penalty, Page 56.

Fight Rule

- When any team member or personnel causes physical abuse to an opponent by striking with their arms, hands, feet, legs, or equipment while fighting or spits at their opponent, they are subject to the following:

  Rule 5: Section: 16-a, Page 54.

  Penalties:

  1. First offense: Ejection plus a four-game suspension.
  2. Second offense in the same season: Ejection plus a five-game suspension.
  3. Third offense in the same season: Ejection plus suspension for the remainder of the season and postseason.

  Rule 5: Section: 16-b, Penalty a-b-1), Page 54.

- When any team member or personnel causes physical abuse to an umpire or game official by any threat of physical intimidation or harm by pushing, shoving, contact, kicking dirt, spitting, spraying, throwing at, or attempting to make physical contact towards the umpire or official, they are subject to the following:

  Rule 5: Section: 16-b, 56.

  Penalties:

  1. First offense: Ejection plus a four-game suspension.
  2. Second offense in the same season: Ejection plus a five-game suspension.
  3. Third offense in the same season: Ejection plus suspension for the remainder of the season and postseason.

  Rule 5: Section: 16-b, Penalty a-b-1), Page 54.

Ejection Rulings

- Any violation of the Coaches' and Players' Code of Ethics listed on the last page of this chapter is an ejection.
    1. On a first offense, the umpire may give an official warning to the offending player, coach, or team before ejecting.

Rule 3: Section: 6-d, Page 37.

- Umpires have authority over anyone negatively affecting the enforcement of the rules and penalties.
    1. A player, coach, or team attendant must comply when asked by the umpire to either do something or stop doing something.

Rule 3: Section: 6-a, Page 37.

- An ejected individual must leave the field immediately.

Rule 3: Section: 6-d, Note 2, Page 37 – 38.

1. The ejected individual is not allowed to either communicate, be heard from in any way, or be in visual sight of the teams or umpires for the remainder of the contest.

Rule 3: Section: 6-d, Note 2, Page 37 – 38.

2. Only after the umpiring crew is escorted from the field can the ejected individual return to the confines of the field.

Rule 3: Section: 6-d, Note 3, Page 38.

Penalty: In addition to an ejection or a post-game ejection, a three-game suspension is given to the offender for violation of this rule.

Rule 6: Section: 3-d, Penalty, Notes 2 – 3, Page 38.

- When the head coach is ejected, he is replaced by a substitute head coach. When the substitute head coach gets ejected, in addition to being ejected, that substitute head coach serves a one-game suspension.

Rule 2: Section: 26-g, Page 24.

Offensive Coach and Team Rulings

- Only the base coaches, batter, on-deck batter, and runners are allowed out of the dugout during live-ball play.

  Note: This rule applies even during pitching changes.

  Rule 5: Section: 2-c, Note, Page 44.

  Penalties:

  1. First offense: Warning.
  2. Second offense: Ejection.

  Rule 5: Section: 2-c, Penalty, Page 44.

- Uniformed team members or coaches cannot stand near or behind home plate or the backstop while the pitcher is either warming up or pitching.

  Rule 5: Section: 2-e, Page 44.

  Penalties:

  1. First offense: Warning to move.
  2. When they do not immediately move, ejection.

  Rule 5: Section: 2-e, Penalty, Page 44.

- The on-deck batter must be near his dugout.

  Penalties:

  1. First offense: Warning to move.
  2. No immediate movement: Ejection.

  Rule 5: Section: 2-e, Penalty, Page 44.

- When a home run is hit, no one may leave the warning track area—a 15 foot distance beyond the dugout—to celebrate other than the on-deck batter or baserunners.

  Rule 5: Section: 2-d, Page 44.

  Penalties:

  1. First offense: Warning.
  2. Second offense: Ejection.

  Rule 5: Section: 2-d, Penalty, Page 44.

- Umpires keep coaches and their personnel in their designated dugout bench, bull pen, or dead-ball territory while the ball is in play.

Rule 3: Section: 8-d, Page 39 – 40.

Penalties:

1. First offense: Warning.
2. Second offense: Ejection.

Rule 3: Section: 8-d, Penalty, Page 39 – 40.

Code of Ethics

- Coaches are responsible for controlling their players and preventing any unsportsmanlike actions that their players may show towards opponents, officials, or spectators.
- Coaches must obey all rules.
- It is the coach's obligation to teach his players to be respectful and show dignity to the game of baseball, officials, opponents, and schools they represent.
- Coaches can only discuss rule interpretations, but they cannot question umpire's judgement.
- Coaches cannot allow their players to make personal malicious remarks, cursing, or obscene language towards opponents, umpires, or spectators.
- Coaches cannot cause or encourage unsportsmanlike actions from players or spectators.
- Umpires are expected to be courteous and dignified towards coaches and players.
- Coaches can get help from school authorities to control uncontrollable students or spectators.

Page 8.

Acknowledgements

Mr. **Billy Haze** understands that anything that can greatly improve an umpire's ability to retain and apply the rules of college baseball more easily, correctly and faster is a good thing.

I have seen firsthand the positive impact he has had on hundreds of umpires from all across the country. Billy's solid commitment to help others improve their knowledge and professionalism as umpires is a true test of his character as a person. Billy has also heard and agrees with the opinions expressed by hundreds of umpires everywhere the need for a better baseball rules resource. Thanks to Mr. Billy Haze for all the encouragement and endorsing the *Baseball Rules in Black and White* series.

About the Author

After five decades of either playing, coaching, or umpiring the game of baseball, **James C. Bettencourt** decided to write a series of books called *Baseball Rules in Black and White*. While umpiring over the last two decades, James has ruled on thousands of plays. He has an umpire's perspective knowing which rules are frequently called during games. What James also knows was that just because a ruling is frequently called in a game does not mean those rules have been accurately interpreted.

For umpire James C. Bettencourt—after a lifetime of baseball, two decades of umpiring, dozens of camps, clinics, and many mentors—his own personal baseball rule knowledge and application of those rules was not acceptable to him.

So beginning in the winter of 2015, James set out to make an optimum-learning series for the most frequently called rules in the game of baseball for each specific level of play. As a result, in the fall of 2016, the first in the series of *Baseball Rules in Black and White* was released, *Difficult High School*

Baseball Rules Made Easy. These books improve existing rule book language with accurate and easy to read sentences, which are easy to locate and are written in big font.